Recapturing Wisdom's Valley

THE WATERVLIET SHAKER HERITAGE, 1775–1975

by Dorothy M. Filley

EDITED BY MARY L. RICHMOND

PUBLISHED BY THE TOWN OF COLONIE AND THE ALBANY INSTITUTE OF HISTORY AND ART
UNDER A GRANT FROM THE ALBANY CITY AND COUNTY BICENTENNIAL COMMISSION
ON THE OCCASION OF AN EXHIBITION CELEBRATING THE BICENTENNIAL OF SHAKER SETTLEMENT

Frontispiece: *Worldly curiosity of the 1860s produced a crush of Sabbathday visitors' carriages at the Shakers' Great Gate. For almost fifty years a stream of visitors came to Wisdom's Valley on the Sabbath, when the Great Gate was open. A diary entry dated 8 August 1852 estimated visitors' carriages at 144. The following week's entry was "over 150 carriages at meeting today; 200 people could not get in." As late as 1885,* Frank Leslie's Monthly *described the scene as comprising "high-steppers and landaus, village carts and farmers' wagons, natty avenue omnibuses, and rudely impro- vised buses and old diligences, with flapping black curtains." There were many times, however, when the Shakers had to withdraw their hospitality — and close the Great Gate — because of thoughtless actions of the world. (New York State History Collection)*

Right: *Spirit drawing, Watervliet, 28 April 1845 (detail). The identity of the Watervliet Shaker who sent the letter containing this spirit drawing to Molly Smith at Hancock in 1847 is unknown. The drawing documents a spirit of communication sent in 1845 to Molly Smith by Isreal Hammond, who had died six years before. (Library of The United Society of Shakers, Sabbathday Lake, Maine)*

Covers: *Early twentieth-century photograph (front) and 1860s stereopticon pair (back) from the New York State History Collection. Cover design by Edward J. Deniega.*

Library of Congress Cataloging in Publication Data

Filley, Dorothy M.
    Recapturing Wisdom's Valley.
    Published on the occasion of an exhibition celebrating the bicentennial of Shaker settlement.
    1. Shakers — Watervliet, N.Y. — Exhibitions.
2. Watervliet, N.Y. — History — Exhibitions. I. Title
BX9768.W2F53   289.8'0974'42   75-27133
ISBN 0-89062-010-5

Produced by Publishing Center for Cultural Resources, 27 West 53 Street, New York City 10021.

Manufactured in the United States of America.

The writing and publishing of this record of our Albany County Shakers is most gratifying. It is a contribution to the history of our area that is truly significant and a most fitting undertaking of the Bicentennial.

Much that is very good will come from this book. The lives of our children and their children will be better because of the example set by the Shakers so beautifully described here.

My congratulations to the author and to the committee responsible for the publication.

Erastus Corning 2nd, Mayor
City of Albany, New York
3 July 1975

I am pleased with this chronicle of the very important Shaker life in Colonie.

The Shakers would allow no compromise in the quality of their workmanship or products. They were perfectionists. They proved the value of simple, functional design and use of the best, sturdiest materials.

The Shakers were two hundred years ahead of time in their belief in and insistence on applying the concept of equal rights to all human relationships, a concept which is reflected in today's court decisions, legislative enactments, and public attitude.

This volume is more than a catalogue of unique furniture, tools, buildings, and accomplishments. It is a recognition of the greatness of the Shaker philosophy of life, much of which is as valid today as it was in 1775.

William K. Sanford, Supervisor
Town of Colonie, New York
17 June 1975

Preface

My earliest recollection of the Shakers is of their Watervliet cemetery. When we drove by it as children, we always looked to see Mother Ann's stone standing in the center, taller than the rest. It made a lasting impression.

This study of the Watervliet Shakers is cosponsored by the Albany Institute of History and Art and the Town of Colonie. Research, which was made possible through a grant from the New York State Council on the Arts, was begun in July 1974 and culminated in an exhibition opening in September 1975.

Because the history of the Watervliet Shakers has never been written, and because of the importance of Watervliet to Shakerism, the project was undertaken to coincide with the Bicentennial of the United States. *Recapturing Wisdom's Valley* is not only a history of the Watervliet Shakers, but also a catalogue of the exhibition, published by the Town of Colonie and the Albany Institute under a grant from the Albany City and County Bicentennial Commission. It does not purport to be the definitive history of the Shakers at Watervliet, but it is hoped that this chronological record of available data, arranged in twenty-five-year intervals, will be a springboard to the compilation of materials which have not yet been discovered or investigated. The research for this volume has been undertaken in many libraries and museums, and in personal interviews with experts in the field and individuals who knew the Watervliet Shakers. Every attempt has been made to preserve original spelling and punctuation.

I wish to express my sincere gratitude to the multitude of persons who have contributed so generously to this project, and list here those whose assistance has been substantial: Gertrude Cross Adams, Harriet Dyer Adams, Richard S. Allen, James Corsaro, Carrell Devitt, A. Donald Emerich, E. Walter Engel, Douglas Haverly, Virginia Hawley, Lou Willey Hillard, James Hobin, R. Arthur Johnson, Theodore E. Johnson, Victoria Cross Johnson, Marian Curtis Kunz, William L. Lassiter, Richard and Mabel Leadley, Mildred Ledden, Anne Marvin, Robert F. W. Meader, Catherine Cross Millard, John Ott, Elmer R. Pearson, William Pillsbury, John Poppeliers, Marguerite Putnam, Donald Richmond, John Shea, Gertrude Reno Sherburne, Viola Cross Sourdiffe, Francis Spoonogle, George Stedman, John Still, Charles E. Thompson, Julius Tretick, Fred Tribley, Charles and Helen Upton, John Waite, Edith Wasmuth, John Watson, Frank Willey, Mabel Diener Willey, Nellie Oyer Winter, and Peter Wolf.

My sincere thanks go to Erastus Corning, Mayor of the City of Albany, and to William K. Sanford, Supervisor of the Town of Colonie, for their support.

The hospitality of the Shaker sisters will always be remembered: Eldresses Bertha Lindsay and Gertrude Soule and Sister Miriam Wall of Canterbury, New Hampshire; and Sisters Mildred Barker and Frances Carr of Sabbathday Lake, Maine.

My gratitude for their patience and cooperation goes to the two people responsible for my becoming involved in this project: Jean Olton, Historian of the Town of Colonie, and Norman Rice, Director of the Albany Institute of History and Art.

For those most closely involved in this publication my sincere appreciation: to Frederick L. Rath, my former mentor, for his excellent foreword; to M. J. (Mike) Gladstone for his sense of perfection in publication; to Caroline Hightower for her very professional assistance; and lastly, but of the most importance, to Mary L. Richmond who, as editor of *Recapturing Wisdom's Valley*, shared with me her knowledge and understanding of Shakerism together with her research expertise, and supplied references from her manuscript bibliography *Shaker Literature. A Bibliography in Two Parts with Annotations,* to be published in 1976 at the University Press of New England.

D.M.F.
Troy, New York

Shakers pose at the Great Gate in the 1860s.

Foreword

T. S. Eliot once remarked that history has many cunning corridors. One that has had an increasing fascination for us began as the British colonists prepared for a test of strength with their rulers. In the summer of 1774, Ann Lee Standerin came with a small group of her followers to the colony of New York. With Mother Ann, these members of The United Society of Believers in Christ's Second Appearing, known as Shakers, laid foundations for a socioreligious movement that would endure beyond a lifetime.

In the two centuries that have ensued, the Shakers prospered and then waned. Of the more than one thousand Shaker buildings that were erected in communities from Maine to Kentucky, only about 350 survive, many of them altered beyond recognition. A few belong to the handful of remaining Shakers; some have been adapted to other uses; and a few have been preserved.

Recapturing Wisdom's Valley is a study in depth by an acute historian-observer, Dorothy M. Filley, of the first Shaker settlement, Wisdom's Valley, located in the Township of Watervliet in Albany County. Never has so much information about the first settlement been brought together before. It is an accomplishment of major importance in the historiography of the utopian movements in the United States. It may also help to bring about the preservation of some of the remaining structures in the Watervliet community. This, at least, is the hope of those who believe that it is good for a people to save for themselves and for future generations the most significant sites, buildings, and objects in their history and culture.

State and federal interest in the Watervliet Shaker community has been intermittent. Dr. Charles C. Adams, who was named director of the New York State Museum in 1926, and one of his assistants,

William Lassiter, undertook to collect Shaker materials, and for a period they worked with Edward Deming Andrews, who had become an authority on the subject. In 1973 on the recommendation of the Board for Historic Preservation and the State Historic Preservation Officer, the United States Department of the Interior placed the newly formed Watervliet-Shaker Historic and Recreation District on the National Register of Historic Places.

The district comprises over 510 acres, including an historic area in which some twenty-five original buildings still remain and an archaeological area in which there are remains dating back to the 1790s. About 60 percent of the land is now privately owned; the rest is owned by Albany County. As Peter Wolf, planning consultant, has pointed out, it is valuable land directly in the path of expansion of the burgeoning community of Colonie, New York. His *Land Management Study* is the basis for the drawings which conclude this volume.

The town has considered taking advantage of state and federal funding to acquire the privately held land to insure preservation in perpetuity. Mrs. Jean Olton, Town Historian, has taken the lead in the preservation movement.

This exhibition demonstrates that the values cherished by the Shakers, summed up in one of their principal songs, "The Gift to Be Simple," might be found again by generations whose lives are often confused and complex. Beyond fascination for their crafts, their arts, there is something more about the Shakers — perhaps a dream, fatally flawed and never quite realized, but often with a purity that suggests the endless quest by imperfect humans for perfection.

Ultimately, what the Shaker movement suggests — and what is here demonstrated — is a paradox: the success of failure, a distance of mind and meaning.

Frederick L. Rath
Deputy Commissioner for Historic Preservation
New York State Office of Parks and Recreation
23 June 1975

James Irving, who took the preceding photograph, made this additional 1860s record of brethren within the Great Gate and immediately in front of the original, Church Family, quadrangle. (New York State History Collection)

9

A
CONCISE STATEMENT
OF THE
PRINCIPLES,
OF THE
ONLY TRUE CHURCH,
ACCORDING TO
THE GOSPEL
OF THE
PRESENT APPEARANCE
OF
CHRIST.

As held to and practised upon by the true
followers of the LIVING SAVIOUR,
at NEWLEBANON, &c.

TOGETHER WITH A LETTER FROM
JAMES WHITTAKER,
Minister of the Gospel in this day of CHRIST's
second appearing—to his natural relations in
England. Dated October 9th, 1785.

Printed at Bennington, Vermont,
By HASWELL & RUSSELL—1790.

Recapturing Wisdom's Valley

Wisdom's Valley is a nineteenth-century spiritual name for the first of the Shaker communities that constituted the most successful experiment in communitarianism in America. It was here that Mother Ann Lee established the Shakers in 1776, and where she died in 1784. She is buried in the Shaker cemetery, one of the few remaining traces that this historic community existed.

When the Shakers first settled the area it was known by its Indian name, *Nis-ka-yu-na* ("extended corn flats"), and was part of the Manor Rensselaerwyck. It became the town of Watervliet when townships were first laid out in Albany County, and it was redesignated as the Town of Colonie by the legislature in 1895, which it remains today. The Shakers gave their own spiritual name to it in 1850.

In order to recapture Wisdom's Valley, we must rely on the accounts of those who visited the community, the diaries and records of the Shakers themselves, the remembrances of those who either knew or lived with the Shakers, and a great deal of legend in the sense that legend is "a narrative, usually entertaining, based on tradition with some intermixture of fact, springing up naturally among a people and unconsiously embodying popular feeling."[1]

A mixture of legend and fact tells us that Ann Lees (the *s* was later dropped from her name) was born on Toad Lane in Manchester, England, in 1736. Uneducated and illiterate, she worked in the industrial mills as a child. With a tendency toward religious mysticism, this sober young woman joined Jane and James Wardley, former Quakers, who worshiped with shouting, singing, and dancing which prompted the de-

This 1790 pamphlet, written by Father Joseph Meacham, was the first printed publication issued by the Shakers. For earlier references to the Shakers it is necessary to rely on travelers' accounts or the writings of apostates. Father Joseph was responsible for gathering the Believers into families as well as strongly ordered societies. (Henry Francis duPont Winterthur Museum, Edward Deming Andrews Memorial Shaker Collection)

rogatory designation as Shaking Quakers. Possibly persuaded by her family, Ann married Abraham Standerin, a blacksmith (as was her father), and bore four children who died in infancy. She became very active in the Wardleys' society for several years, and was eventually looked on as its spiritual leader.

Probably because of her own tragic experience as a mother, she believed that the "lusts of the flesh" were the cause of the world's problems. Following years of persecution and imprisonment in England for her eccentric manner of worship, a vision led to her decision to establish the Shakers in America.

Consequently, Ann Lee and a small group of followers left England and sailed on the *Mariah,* landing in America on 6 August 1774. In this group were Ann Lee and her husband (who abandoned her soon after), John Hocknell and his son Richard, James Whittaker, Mary Partington, James Shepherd, and Ann Lee's niece Nancy Lees and brother William.

The Shakers believed in a dual Messiah and that Ann Lee, their leader, was the female Messiah; they called her Mother Ann. The principal tenets of their belief at this time were confession of sins and celibacy. Their formal name was (and is) The United Society of Believers in Christ's Second Appearing. In time the Believers were addressed individually as Father, Brother, and Sister.

1775–1800

The history of Wisdom's Valley begins in 1775, when three of the Believers (John Hocknell, William Lee, and James Whittaker), upon hearing of cheap land near Albany, set out for the Manor Rensselaerwyck to investigate. At some time during the year John Hocknell, who had financed the journey from England, leased a farm of 200 acres about three-quarters of a mile north of the present Albany County Ann Lee Home. Leaving Lee and Whittaker, who found work in Albany at their respective trades of blacksmith and weaver, Hocknell went back to England — returning with John (husband of Mary) Partington, his own family, and money to pay for the property. Although they arrived in this country on Christmas Day of 1775, it was not until several months later that all the Believers were reunited at Niskayuna. Here, living in a small log house, they endured their first hardships in this country. While trying to subdue the stumps and bogs on their land, a combination of swamp and dense forest, they waited passively for converts to their religion.

One of many accounts concerning the first years at Niskayuna, recorded in the 1847 journal of Prudence Morrill, fixes the location of the first dwelling house:

"I have before remarked that the first purchase was about one mile north of the present location of the Church family;* this purchase did not embrace the site now occupied by their buildings. However soon after removing to the place already bought Mother Ann had a feeling to move into the little cabin already spoken of as standing where the Church now stands: This was affected without much difficulty as the proprietor Vanransalare [Van Rennselaer] had already offered them a tract of land some miles in extent for a small rent. . . . Through the agency of John Hocknell, Mother Ann's desire was accomplished in the year 1777."[2]

Another report about the first dwelling house, written in 1828 by a former Shaker, W. J. Haskett, states that the Believers lived in their first "log-hut for three and one-half years," until 1780, before moving to the permanent Church Family site.[3]

Apostate Thomas Brown in his book, *An Account of the People Called Shakers* (published by the author in Troy in 1812), stated that Partington and Hocknell each contracted for a small farm. A document of 1779 shows that Partington was taxed (probably as agent for the Shakers) for land which could have encompassed both properties. The original lease to the Shakers was not recorded and has never been located. Although referred to by Shaker historians as a lease from Stephen Van Rensselaer, the document would have been signed by Catharine Van Rensselaer, widow of Stephen Van Rensselaer II, or the executors of his estate. Stephen Van Rensselaer II died in 1769, and Abraham Ten Broeck became the executor of his estate and guardian of Stephen Van Rensselaer III. Ten Broeck, who later became the mayor of Albany, delivered all patents, deeds, and legal documents to the patroon when he became twenty-one years of age in 1786. The Shakers were reported to have rented their lands from the patroon at "8 Bushells of wheat for every 100 acres"[4] like other early Van Rensselaer leases, which stipulated rentals in terms of wheat by bushel or skipple (.764 bushel).

David Austin Buckingham, Shaker and historian of the Watervliet Church Family, listed in an 1825 report that the first dwelling house was built ("in first Mother's day") in 1778, a second house in 1783, an addition to the first dwelling house in 1784, and the "Old Log meeting house" in 1784.[5] If Buckingham's figures are at all accurate, there is reason to assume that the settlement at the site of the Church Family in 1778 may have followed a break in the financial situation of the small group, as they were hired the same year by the city of Albany to carry donations to the victims of a famine at Lake George some sixty miles distant.

Although they were not actively proselyting in these early years, there was one convert to the new religion. Eleanor Vedder, a neighbor, became the first "outside" Shaker — or one espousing Shaker principles but not living within the Shaker community — about 1779. She is not buried at Wisdom's Valley, but four of her five granddaughters — Eleanor, Catharine, Clarissa, and Polly — died in the faith and are buried in the community cemetery.

---

*The community eventually numbered four families, which were named in geographic relationship to the first, or Church, family. Thus Wisdom's Valley was ultimately the home of a Church Family, a North Family, a South Family, and a West Family.

By 1780, as Mother Ann had prophesied, the first visitors to the new sect began to appear, and some became converts. As a result of disappointment over a well-publicized but unfulfilled religious prophecy in New Lebanon (failure of the appearance of the Messiah) many came to Niskayuna to investigate the new religion. Among these was Joseph Meacham, a Baptist lay preacher from Enfield, Connecticut, later to become the spiritual leader of Shakerism. He and Hocknell, while going to the defense of David Darrow (unjustly accused of driving a flock of sheep to the enemy) were arrested on 7 July 1780 and imprisoned.

Actually Darrow was driving the sheep from Lebanon to the Shakers at Watervliet and resisted the questioning of the authorities, who, with the revolutionary war in progress, were suspicious of and misinterpreted the pacifism of the Shakers. Two weeks after the arrest of Meacham and Hocknell, John Partington, William Lee, James Whittaker, Mary Partington, and Mother Ann (all British), were imprisoned in Albany for "daily dissuading the friends to the American cause from taking up Arms in defence of their Liberties." During the month of August, Mother Ann and Mary Partington were separated from the others and "sent down to the Commissioners at Poughkeepsie for the purpose of their being removed within the Enemies Lines."[6] All the others were released on bail in November, and finally Mother Ann was pardoned by Gov. George Clinton and released on the bonds of William Lee and James Whittaker on 4 December 1780.

News of the release of Mother Ann helped to bring more visitors to Niskayuna, and many were converted to Shakerism including the followers of Meacham. By the spring of 1781, the cause had been strengthened to justify a missionary journey through New England despite the fact that the Revolution still was in progress. Accompanied by William Lee, James Whittaker, Samuel Fitch, Mary Partington, and Margaret Leland,

Mother Ann set out on her "incredible journey."[7] The tour was fraught with dangers, persecution, and deprivation. Many were converted during the journey that lasted for two years and four months.

The physical punishment endured on the missionary tour by Father William Lee and Mother Ann probably brought about their deaths, less than two months apart. Mother Ann's obituary was published in *The Albany Gazette,* 9 September 1784: "Departed this life, at Nisquenia, Sept. 7, Mrs. Lee, known by the appellation of the *Elect Lady* or *Mother of Zion,* and head of that people called Shakers. Her funeral is to be attended this day."[8]

Following the death of Mother Ann, Father James Whittaker was chosen to be the spiritual leader of Shakerism. At this point there was some unrest among the Believers. Members of the original group terminated their association with the sect, or "left," for various reasons: James Shepherd and John Partington refused to serve under Whittaker's leadership; Richard Hocknell and Nancy Lees, the niece of Mother Ann, left and were subsequently married.

The earliest known foreign reference to the Shakers at Niskayuna is in the diary of Francisco de Miranda, a Venezuelan serving in the American Revolution, who visited the settlement in 1783 in the company of several military officials. He said about his visit, "The house, or site, is called the Gate of Heaven and they refer to themselves as The Sons of God."[9]

There is also an interesting legend concerning the Marquis de Lafayette at Niskayuna. It tells of his visit to a Shaker meeting, his attempt to mesmerize a Shaker, and an interview with Mother Ann herself. As a student of Mesmer, the Viennese physician, Lafayette was interested in the Shakers' possible ability to exhibit animal magnetism — as they professed that they could heal disease by the "laying on of hands." Lafayette was in Albany in 1784 on his way to a meeting to make peace with the Indians. His party stopped at Niskayuna and attended church services, but the details of the story are not easily credited and the reported date of the visit was actually three weeks after Mother Ann's death.[10]

Joseph Meacham, whom Mother Ann had called "her first-born son in America," became the male spiritual leader of the Shakers in 1787 after the death of Father James Whittaker. He selected Mother Lucy Wright as the female leader. Although Father Joseph lived only a short time as the leader of Shakerism, he left the Believers with a strongly structured form of government based on the four tenets of their belief: confession of sins, celibacy, separation from the outside community, or "world," and common ownership of property. Besides these tenets the Shakers believed in equality of the sexes, the absence of racial discrimination, pacifism, and devotion to industry and perfection. Many later observers felt that it was Father Joseph's formulation of doctrine that made Shaker communitarianism as successful as it was.

By 1787, however, Niskayuna was no longer to be the center of Shaker spiritual guidance. New Lebanon became the first organized society of Believers, and in 1787 Niskayuna became the second Shaker society organized with the main authority vested in the Central Ministry at New Lebanon. The regions were divided into bishoprics: New Lebanon and Watervliet were in the same bishopric. Each family in a society was governed by a system of elders and eldresses, deacons and deaconesses, and both male and female trustees. Two elders and two eldresses, of equal status, were responsible for the spiritual affairs of the members of each family. These families were independent economic orders whose temporal affairs were managed by the deacons and trustees, deacons being responsible for industrial activities and the trustees for all financial involvements.

Between 1785 and 1788 a young man named St. John Honeywood visited the Shakers at Niskayuna more than once during his stay in Albany as a law student. His posthumously published volume of poetry and prose leaves us the following descriptions:

"I was pleased with the cleanly simplicity of every object . . . and when I first beheld the mystic dance; five or six women were whirling round on the floor with a velocity almost inconceivable . . . one woman spun for 30 minutes without becoming dizzy. . . . The last summer, upon another excursion, I found forty or fifty dancing at once . . . they suggested the idea of a throng of discontented ghosts hovering round the gloomy shores of the Stygian lake. . . . The Magistrates of the State of *New-York* have behaved with wisdom in taking no notice of them: neglected, they will sink to nothing; persecuted, they will certainly increase."[11]

It may well be that many prominent Americans first heard about the Shakers through the publication of Honeywood's description. The extensive list of subscribers who received the small volume included Aaron Burr, Gov. George Clinton, DeWitt Clinton, Alexander Hamilton, John Jay, Robert Livingston, and Stephen Van Rensselaer.

The only public records to give clues to the extent of early Shaker holdings at Niskayuna are the Albany County tax lists. In 1786, against the northwest district quota of £14,920, John Hackney[Hocknell] and sons are shown to have property valued at £16, William Lee's place is valued at £7, and James Shepherd, James Wittaker [Whittaker], and John Partington are shown with evaluations of £9 each. Stephen Van Rensselaer's holdings are valued at £2,872.[12]

The first United States census, in 1790, gives us an official head count of the Watervliet community, but since it does not record Shakers as such, one must rely on individual names for information. David Meacham appears with a family of nineteen males over age sixteen, nine females over sixteen, and five more under sixteen. Hezekiah Noble's family totals twenty-one.[13] The census shows Richard Hocknell, as the head of a family, living apart from the Shakers. The same is true of John Partington, although we know that his wife, Mary Partington, remained with the Shakers and is buried at Watervliet.

We can deduce from the census that there were two Shaker families, with Hezekiah Noble and David Meacham as leaders. (Elders were not appointed at Watervliet until 1793.) The two must have been the First Order of the Church Family, commonly called the Church Family, and the Second Order, or North Family. The Second Order may have been formed as a backsliding order. Thomas Brown mentioned Believers who left the Shakers and later returned, living apart in a "backsliding order."[14]

David Austin Buckingham, in his "Epitomic History of the Watervliet Shakers," tells us that the pattern for the agricultural and industrial growth of the community was set by 1790, "when Believers . . . had a family garden, occupying about two acres of land." Under Joseph Turner's supervision, he relates, they began to raise a few seeds for sale, although previously "it was not customary in this part of the country to raise garden seeds to vend." When broomcorn was first introduced at Watervliet in 1791, he tells us, considerable attention was paid to its cultivation with "brooms . . . manufactured for market purposes, and sold at the fair price of half a dollar each."[15] Brooms later became a flourishing industry after the invention of the first flat broom by Brother Theodore Bates at Watervliet in 1799.

The construction of buildings proceeded steadily at the rate of one a year, and from the journal of a temporary resident in Albany County, we learn the extent of the Shaker building and industry in 1795. La Marquise de la Tour du Pin and her husband, members of the court of Marie Antoinette who sought refuge in this country during the French Revolution, lived for two years at what is now the intersection of Watervliet Shaker Road and Delatour Road. The lady recorded that "a nice wagon, loaded with fine vegetables, often passed before our door. It belonged to the Shakers, who were located at a distance of six or seven miles. The driver of the wagon always stopped at our house, and I never failed to talk with him about their manner of life, their customs, and their belief."[16]

Of a subsequent visit to the Shakers, she wrote of "a large number of nice wooden houses, a church, schools, and a community house of brick," and mentioned a "superb kitchen-garden with everything in a state of the greatest prosperity, but without the least evidence of elegance" as well as immense community stables, dairies, factories for the production of butter and cheese, and the neat, uniform appearance of the gray wool homespun costumes of the men, women, and children. Everywhere she observed order and absolute silence. "Through the windows," she wrote, "we could see the looms of the weavers, and the pieces of cloth which they were dyeing, also the workshops of the tailors and the dress-makers. But not a word or a song was to be heard anywhere."[17]

The marquise noted that the Shaker who sold vegetables was not willing to accept money from her hand, suggesting the Millennial Laws of future years which forbade men and women to touch each other.

Another very early journal describing the "Shaking Quakers" was kept by the traveler Moses Guest. Despite some ambiguities (his entry dated Sunday, 10 October 1796 describes a log meetinghouse — whereas the 1791 meetinghouse was of frame construction) he presents a very believable picture of a building "50 feet in length, and 25 in width, with a chimney at each end. When I entered this building," he wrote, "I beheld 24 men dancing at one end of the room and 20 women at the other. They appeared to be from the age of 14 to 80 years; and were formed four deep. Two of their elders were singing a song . . . called the rose tree."[18]

New York State records show that the first burial in the community cemetery was in 1797, but reinterment records of 1835 account for three prior burials, and recently discovered data show six burials before 1797, the earliest being that of Violet Bennett (age 25) in 1785.

Thomas Brown, although an apostate a valuable source of early information about the community, visited the Shakers in 1798 after being intrigued by an inflammatory pamphlet written by Valentine Rathbun. In Watervliet he talked with Benjamin Youngs, who had joined the sect in 1792 and had lived as an outside Shaker with his own family. Youngs persuaded him to visit the large Shaker families to see "what union, love, peace, and quietness prevailed among them."[19] Favorably impressed, Brown became a novitiate member in 1798, influencing Ralph Hodgson and William Carter to also join. In Cornwall, New York, where he lived, Brown subsequently debated and preached diligently for Shakerism.

The first New York State law written expressly for the Shakers was a 1798 statute allowing an affirmation to substitute for an oath in a court of law. When Brown had asked Youngs, "What is your faith and practice concerning swearing before the civil magistrate?" Youngs had replied, "Our faith and practice is according to the precept of Christ, *Not to Swear at all* . . . but to let our communication be yea, yea and nay, nay: for whatsoever is more than these, cometh of evil."[20] The New York State "Act for the relief of the people called Shaking Quakers, and the religious sect known by the name of 'Universal Friends'" extends to them the privilege formerly afforded to the Quakers.[21]

The first deeds involving the Shakers recorded in the Albany County Clerk's office are indexed under names that include Society of Shakers, Shakers Society, United Shakers Society, United Society of People called Shakers, United Society called Shakers or commonly called Shakers. In the first of these deeds, dated 2 November 1799 and recorded on the twenty-ninth, Benjamin Young[s] and his wife, Mary, "in consideration of one dollar and the love and good will which we have for the Society," grants to the Society of Shakers 100 acres in the northwest part of their homestead farm for the "purpose of building houses and a foundation for relief and help of . . . the poorer members of the said Society . . . the poor, the widows and fatherless of this world as may be real objects of charity."[22]

Detail of "A Map of the Manor Renselaerwick," dated 1767. The arrow indicates uninhabited terrain between the Hudson and Mohawk Rivers — the area of swamp and forest which Mother Ann and the first Believers settled ten years later, in 1776.

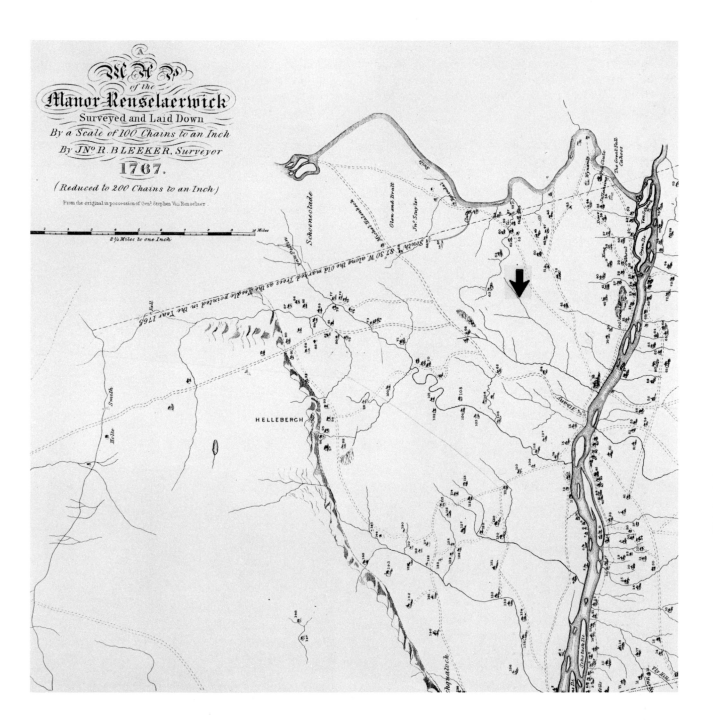

A
MAP
of the
Manor Rensselaerwick
Surveyed and Laid Down
By a Scale of 100 Chains to an Inch
By JNº R. BLEEKER, Surveyor
1767.
(Reduced to 200 Chains to an Inch)

From the original in possession of Genl. Stephen Van Rensselaer.

2½ Miles to one Inch

HELLEBERGH

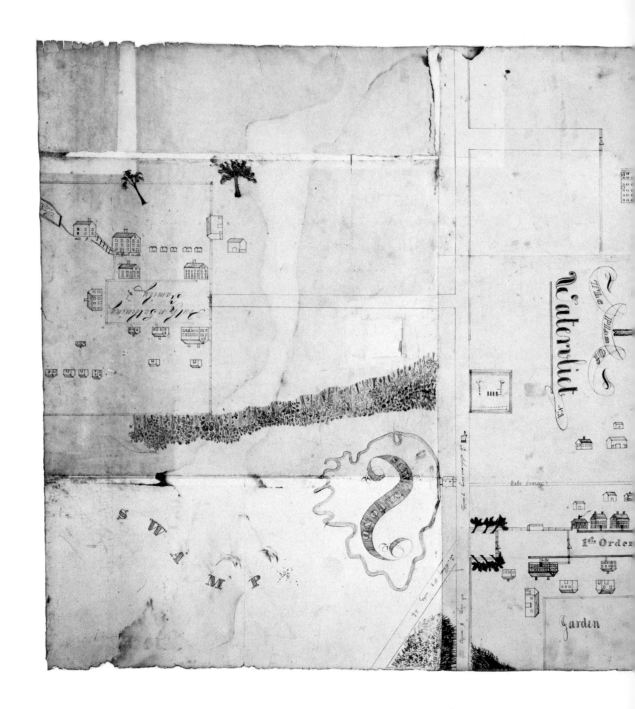

SWAMP

The Plan of Watervliet

1st Order

Garden

18

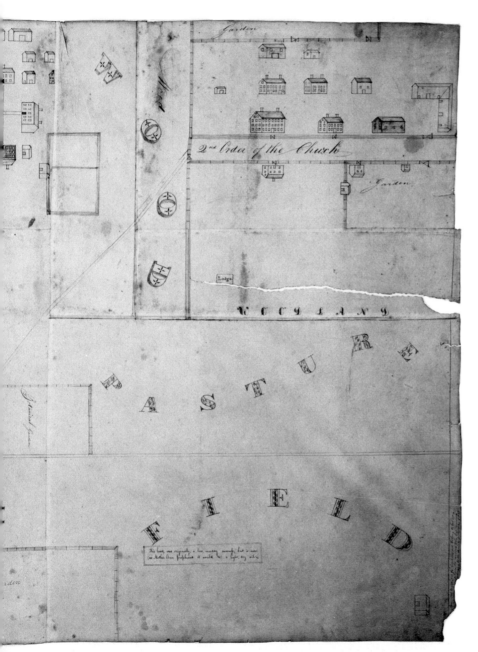

"The Plan of Watervliet, N.Y." The large (27" x 48") uncompleted map, dated 1839 but unsigned, closely resembles the work of David Austin Buckingham, a member of the Watervliet Shaker community at that time. It is the only known map showing all four of the Watervliet families, but they are designated as "1st Order" (Church Family), "2nd Order of the Church" (North Family), "South or Gathering Family" (South Family), and the "2nd Family" (West Family). The legend in the "field" north of the "1st Order" reads: "This land, was originally, a low muddy swamp, but it is now (as Mother Ann prophesied it would be) a light, dry soil." A marginal notation in the torn lower right corner (in the northeast area presently occupied by the Albany County Airport) reveals that "[Mother] Ann was buried, but the land did not belong to believers. . . . to have her removed & she was removed [to land] belonging to the Society in the Spring of 1835." The "burying ground" shown in the center of the map is where Mother Ann's grave was relocated. (Albany Institute of History and Art)

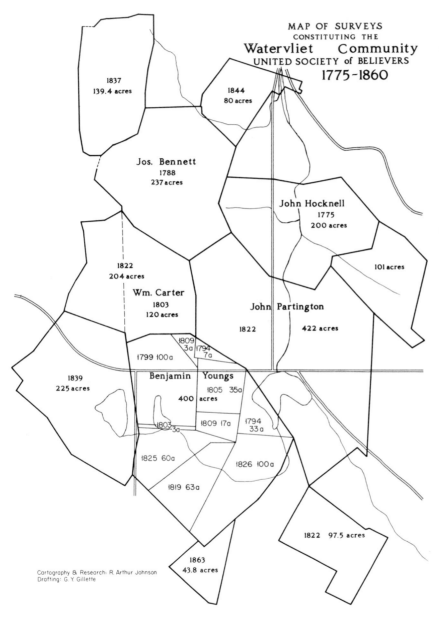

MAP OF SURVEYS
CONSTITUTING THE
Watervliet Community
UNITED SOCIETY of BELIEVERS
1775-1860

1837
139.4 acres

1844
80 acres

Jos. Bennett
1788
237 acres

John Hocknell
1775
200 acres

101 acres

1822
204 acres

Wm. Carter
1803
120 acres

John Partington

1822   422 acres

1809 3a 1794 7a

1799 100a

1839
225 acres

Benjamin Youngs

1805 35a
400 acres

1809 17a 1794 33a

1803 3a

1825 60a

1826 100a

1819 63a

1822   97.5 acres

1863
43.8 acres

Cartography & Research: R. Arthur Johnson
Drafting: G. Y. Gillette

The contiguous properties which constituted the village of the Watervliet Shakers are shown in this map of Van Rensselaer leases. The names shown are those of lessees who conveyed their property to The United Society of Believers. Parcels not bearing names are identified solely by date of Shaker acquisition and acreage. The horizontal road is today's New York State Route 155, and today's Albany-Shaker road is shown as a vertical strip that strikes off to the right below 155, alongside the Ann Lee Pond.

Joseph Bennett (an outside Shaker) leased the parcel of 237 acres bearing his name from Stephen Van Rensselaer in 1788. He and his heirs gradually conveyed this acreage to the Shakers.

Records show only that in 1803 William Carter, also an outside Shaker, leased 120 acres of the 204-acre parcel conveyed to the Shakers in 1822.

There is no deed for the leasing of 200 acres by John Hocknell (as agent for the Shakers) in 1775, but references to the property in Hocknell's name appear in subsequent deeds.

Alvin Boettcher, a local Shaker historian, believed that the parcel of 422 acres which bears John Partington's name (as agent for the Shakers) was leased by Partington as 436.6 acres in 1775. The earliest public record of this as Shaker property (in Partington's name) is dated 1779, but this is the land on which the Church Family was established in 1778. The 1822 date refers to a trustee's reassignment to the Shakers.

The 400 acres bearing Benjamin Youngs's name were bought by him outright rather than leased. He and his heirs gradually conveyed this acreage to the Shakers at the dates indicated on each small parcel (where "a" = acreage). (Historical Society of the Town of Colonie Collection)

Persons Names	Value of Real Estate	Amount of Tax
Anthony Van Schaick	2500	125 ..
Johannes I Lansing	800	40 ..
Dirck Freemstraat	900	45 ..
Cornelius Ouderkerk	400	20 ..
Jacob Ft Lansing	650	32 10
Abraham Ft Lansing	550	27 10
Henry Oothoudt	1800	55 ..
Volkert Oothoudt	1300	65 ..
Carried over		£ 420 ..

Land Tax List of the North West Quarter of the Manor of Rensselaer District in the County of Albany Pursuant to the Directions of an act of the Legislature of the State of New York Intitled an act for Raising Monies by Tax to be applied toward the public exigencies of the State passed 2d Day of March 1799

Brought over	£ 1465	15
Lucas Witbeck	800	40 ..
Lodewick Hendricus	50	2 10
John Partington	350	17 10
Staats Van Santvoort	600	30 ..
Abraham Bovie	250	12 10
Mattias F Bovie	500	25 ..
Andries Meyer	300	15 ..
Andries Meyer Jun	60	3 ..
John Freemstraat Jun	400	20 ..
Hendrick Flerker	200	10 ..
Hendrick Young	70	3 10
Widow Fretts	350	17 10
Jacob Van Olynda	350	17 10
Bastian Tymesa for Land	150	7 10
Bastian Crigier	250	12 10
Martinus Crigier	300	15 ..
Saphrenus Basinger	200	10 ..
Cornelius Monkie	200	10 ..
Dedrick Shaver	400	20 ..
Hendrick Lyker	400	20 ..
William Borough	300	15 ..
Carried forward	£ 1789	15

Brought forward	£ 1789	15
Lodewick Sickel	150	7 10
Dirck De groot	850	42 10
Fredrick Cluet	300	15 ..
Peter Bouman	100	5 ..
William Shilley	10	.. 10
Michal Frooff	100	5 ..
John D Cluett	500	25 ..
Samuel Hagadorn	150	7 10
John Van Auken	100	5 ..
Gerrit Ft Visher	200	10 ..
Fredrick Damyr	60	3 ..
Cornelius De groot	10	.. 10
Abraham De groot	15	.. 15
John Freemstraat	300	15 ..
John Gunsaul	300	15 ..
Peter Gunsaul	300	15 ..
John Gunsaul Jun	300	15 ..
Henry Ostrum	300	15 ..
Benjamin Van Vliet	300	15 ..
Hendrick Gerse	500	25 ..
Nicholas De groot	900	45 ..
Carried over	£ 2077	..

Van Rensselaer land tax list of 1779. Since John Partington's is the only Shaker name which appears, it is reasonable to assume that the common Shaker property valued at £350 was recorded in his name. (New York State Library)

Court House. Lat. 42° 39'.

2. Prison.

Detail of "A Plan of the City of Albany. . ." of 1794. In July 1780, Mother Ann, John Partington, William Lee, James Whittaker, and Mary Partington were charged in this courthouse for "daily dissuading the friends of the American cause from taking up Arms in defence of their Liberties" and were remanded to this prison. (Albany Institute of History and Art)

Letter to Governor Clinton from his brother, James. (New York State Library)

George Clinton was governor of New York State for a total of twenty-one years (the longest term ever served), including the year of Mother Ann's imprisonment. Although no formal pardon is recorded in Clinton's papers, he must have been instrumental in her release and probably took action following this letter from his brother, damaged in the New York State Capitol fire of 1911:

"Albany Nov'r 19th 1780

D'r Sir, The Bearer William Lees, of the Denomination of Shaking Quakers, who has been confined on suspision by the Commissioners here and has been inlarged, has made application to me respecting his sister, Ann Standivin, who, he informs me, has been confined sometime past in or near Poughkeepsie, on a similar account.

"You are better acquainted with the circumstances relating to her, than I can be; you can best determine what is to be done with her, and if nothing material has been proven against her, I shou'd suppose she may [be] released agreeable to their requisition."

Left: *Baltus Van Kleek house, Poughkeepsie, as recorded ca. 1835 by Lossing for the* Pictorial Field-Book of the Revolution. *Mother Ann and Mary Partington were separated from the male prisoners to be removed within enemy lines, but they were never taken beyond Poughkeepsie. They were confined there in the Van Kleek house, which was used as a prison after the burning of the local courthouse at the outbreak of the Revolution.*

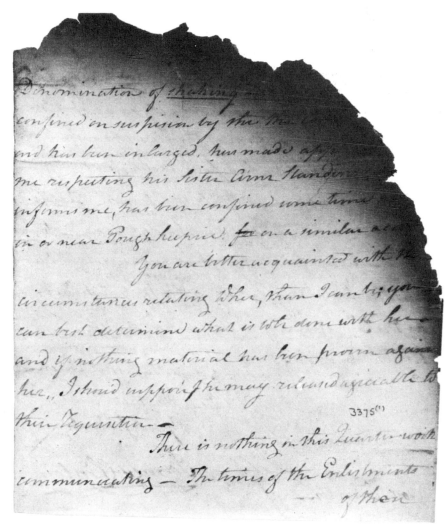

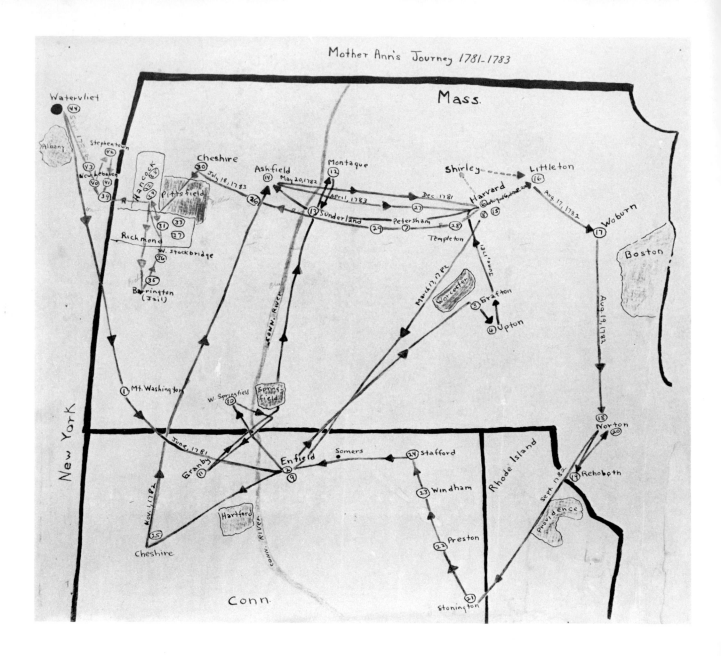

"Mother Ann's Journey 1781–1783" depicts her incredible proselyting tour. The map at left is a good example of a twentieth-century document which has been copied and recopied over the years by many Shakers. (Reproduced courtesy of Marian Curtis Kunz)

First Shaker meetinghouse at Watervliet. Brother Moses Johnson of Enfield, New Hampshire, designed and framed ten such Shaker meetinghouses between 1785 and 1794. He began work on this gambrel-roofed structure for the Watervliet Church Family in March 1791, staying to supervise the foundation and basic framing. The meetinghouse had two doors, the left one for brethren and the right for sisters. The first floor was used for services, and living quarters for the ministry were located on the second floor — reached by separate stairways for the brethren and sisters. According to the

early Millennial Laws the meetinghouses were the only buildings which could be painted white. Most of the dwelling houses were yellow. Interior walls were white, woodwork, Prussian blue, and floors, yellow-ochre. (Reproduced courtesy of Francis Spoonogle)

1800–1825

Through stamina and devotion to industry, the Shakers had cultivated the original wilderness into attractive and prosperous property by the turn of the century. In twenty-five years the population had grown from twelve to eighty-seven; of these, ten still lived in the out families of Benjamin Youngs and William Carter. The others lived in the Shaker family dwellings, which had increased from the first log house to the communal residences of three separate families: the Church Family, the North Family, and the South Family, or Gathering Order, which was established in 1800 for young Believers, or novitiates.

The movement as a whole was also prospering. In addition to New Lebanon and Watervliet in New York State, the following communities had been organized by 1800: in Massachusetts, Hancock, Harvard, Tyringham, and Shirley; in Connecticut, Enfield; in New Hampshire, Canterbury and Enfield; and in Maine, Alfred and New Gloucester (Sabbathday Lake).

At Watervliet in the spring of 1800 a new dwelling house was raised for young Believers on a lot southwest of and adjoining the Church Family property. The land had been deeded to the Shakers by Benjamin Youngs, Sr. on 24 November 1800. The young Believers moved into the new house under the care of Seth Y. Wells and Benjamin S. Youngs (son of Benjamin Youngs, Sr.). There were eight brethren and eight sisters. The number is verified by Thomas Brown, who also noted two Sabbath assemblies in the public meetinghouse, "the Church Order[,] called the old believers[,] in the afternoon and the young believers in the morning."[23]

Benjamin Youngs, who signed and dated this clock in 1806, was a clockmaker by trade who joined the Shakers in 1792. Youngs and his wife, Mary, lived together as brother and sister — with their natural family, on their own property, as an out family. They deeded part of their property to the Shakers in 1799 for the establishment of the South Family. (National Gallery of Art, Index of American Design)

The census of 1800 lists eighty-seven Shakers including nine children under sixteen years of age. The heads of families are shown as William Carter, Peter Dodge, Benjamin Young[s], Seth Wells, and Samuel Pease.

There was a dramatic increase in converts in this period. One, Issachar Bates, who had served in the revolutionary war and later joined the Shakers, wrote of his early life: "After I was married I went to speculating in goods, horses, cattle, sheep-hogs and everything else a fool could think of or take a notion to." Later, he "was convinced it was the work of God among these Shakers; but I was not ready yet I had married a wife [in 1778], and therefore I could not come." After being licensed as a Baptist preacher, he turned once more to the Shakers and visited Lebanon in 1801. He wrote of that occasion, "We did business quick — I eat quick, and talked quick — and heared quick — and started home quick for I was quickened."

His wife, Lovina, joined the Shakers a year later, and in March 1803 the family (except the two oldest sons) moved to Watervliet. Bates recalled that "I went to work as comfortable as a being could wish for — part of the time out preaching to the world, and visiting those we had gathered, and the rest of the time at work till the year 1805."[24]

Sisters Anna Taylor and Leila White, early twentieth-century historians, reported that Bates brought a family of nine, "followed in rapid succession [by] families numbered by sevens and fives and nines . . . [one] of sixteen . . . in all fourteen families, aggregating 96 members, including one family of seven colored members."[25]

On 16 July 1801 the first covenant gave all temporal powers to the deacons of the community. Covenants have been signed periodically since this time, with signatures added over the years as each new member determined at the age of twenty-one to make this expression of faith.

In 1815, Timothy Dwight, president of Yale College, using the work of Thomas Brown as a reference, wrote of the Shaker movement: "The doctrines are so gross that they can never spread far; while the industry, manual skill, fair dealing, and orderly behaviour of the brotherhood, render them useful members of society."[26]

By 1810 the South Family had outgrown the rest of the society. The census of 1810 shows Seth Wells's family with forty-one members, Levi Peas[e] with twenty-eight, Stephen Wells with thirty-two, and David Osborne with fifty-three. Another dwelling house was built "West of North from South Family on opposite side of the road,"[27] and the young Believers were divided into two families. The new order, called the Second (or West) Family, was under Elder Seth Y. Wells. Calvin Wells had care of the South Family subject to the direction and counsel of the eldership of the Second Family but retained the "gathering gift" responsibility for novitiates.

The names of eleven elders and deacons from Watervliet — Calvin Wells, Stephen Wells, Oliver Train, Seth Y. Wells, Joseph Hodgson, Levi Pease, Peter Dodge, David Osborne, David Meacham, Abiather Babbitt, and Morrell Baker — are appended along with those of New Lebanon Shakers to a document of 1815 citing reasons for brethren's refusing to aid or abet the cause of war by bearing arms, paying fines, hiring substitutes, or rendering any equivalent for military services, and noting that Massachusetts and New Hampshire had exempted Shakers from such activity for many years.[28] Again the state of New York looked with compassion on the Shakers and passed an act for their relief from military service on 29 March 1816.

The legislature's equanimity was short-lived. A *Memorial of James Chapman to the respectable Legislature of the State of New York* of 24 March 1817 explains a Shaker episode that attracted national attention. James Chapman and Eunice Hawley were married in 1804. By 1811 he had left her and their three children because he "found it impossible to live with her in peace."[29] Chapman could not support his family living separately, and in 1814 he and the children joined the Shakers at Watervliet. Eunice also joined, but not finding the life to her liking left, attempting to take the children with her and threatening fire and an act of the legislature if the Shakers did not produce them. Chapman wrote his memorial to exonerate the Shakers.

The seriousness of the situation is revealed in a 16 June 1817 letter to Albert Gallatin from Thomas Jefferson describing an act which, if passed, "will carry us back to the times of the darkest bigotry and barbarism, to find a parallel. Its purport is, that all those who shall *hereafter* join in communion with the religious sect of Shaking Quakers, shall be deemed civilly dead, their marriages dissolved, and all their children and property taken out of their hands."[30]

The Chapman affair was buffeted about for over two years. At one point there were daily editorials in *The Albany Gazette* and an anonymous mock drama, *Indoctum Parliamentum*,[31] was written about the lengthy affair.

The New York State legislature finally passed an act on 14 March 1818 which dissolved the Chapman marriage and granted parents the right to petition the court for the custody of children allegedly held by Shakers. The act also imposed penalties upon Shakers or anyone else secreting a child or carrying a child out of the state. The penalties were removed in 1896, but the basic legislation remained effective as Section 71 of the Domestic Relations Law until May 1975.

An Act to Organize a Militia passed in 1818 made the Shakers liable for a fine of four dollars per man for their military exemption. The Chapman affair publicity undoubtedly brought about this legislative change of attitude, and for the next few years the Shakers petitioned the legislature for relief and refused to pay the fines, arguing that "as our position and practice tend entirely to the promotion of peace and quietness it cannot be considered as either dangerous or inconsistent with the safety and welfare of the State."[32]

Martin Van Buren's autobiography relates an incident in the United States Senate in 1824, when he petitioned in behalf of the "Society of Shakers, residents of my native county" regarding military exemption. (Van Buren came from Columbia County, which adjoins Albany County.) When Rufus King, who violently opposed the petition, called the Shakers "a band of fanatics," and moved to table the petition adding that it would be "justly treated were it thrown *under* the table," Van Buren concurred in the condemnation of the Shakers' religious views, but gave them credit for "their charities, their sobriety and their industry — claiming for their common right to petition Congress for a redress of grievance."[33]

Soon after, an Albany newspaper in 1824 reported that "twelve of the Niskayuna Shakers refusing to perform military duty were committed to jail, but that "the colonel of the regiment on learning of the case, remitted their fines and they were liberated."[34] Charles R. Webster, father of printing in Albany, gave bail for resisting Shakers when they were seized and imprisoned and "left no exertion untried to secure the remission of an iniquitous extortion."[35] But in spite of such support and repeated "memorials" to the legislature, the Shakers never really received relief from fines for military exemption until the Civil War.

Despite their problems with the world, the Shaker community continued to prosper. The French author and illustrator J. Milbert, who visited the Niskayuna Shakers in 1817, characterized farm buildings as "enormous," and commented on the meeting room with unadorned brown walls in which pine spittoons filled with sawdust were regularly distributed. Of the dance, Milbert said, "This ceremony astonished me beyond words, but the most amazing feature was the gravity preserved by both men and women in the midst of their furious dancing." He was impressed by the fact that there were no poor Shakers and accredited this to the fact that they would not tolerate idleness. He described their expressions as tranquil "for, like Stoic philosophers, they take the bitter with the sweet, and display neither joy nor sorrow."[36]

After the death of Father Joseph Meacham in 1796, Mother Lucy Wright became the leader of the Central Ministry. It was she who sent Issachar Bates, John Meacham, and Benjamin S. Youngs as missionaries to Kentucky in 1805 and who authorized the publication of Benjamin S. Young's *Testimony of Christ's Second Appearing*.[37] With Father Joseph, she formulated the precepts which were later set down as the statutes and ordinances of the Millennial Laws.

These laws of 1821, by which the society was ordered, were revised by the Central Ministry in 1845. The Millennial Laws of 1845 are considered by the Shakers today as "a product of that era of spiritual ferment and searching in which they were written . . . the very pattern of whose existence placed . . . nearly intolerable conditions of life upon its membership." The 1845 Millennial Laws were revised in 1860 and again in 1887. *"Orders for the Church of Christ's Second Appearing* is with modifications made as recently as January 23, 1938 still in force with the United Society and like its predecessors is read each year on the second Sunday of January wherever Believers are still gathered in community."[38]

Mother Lucy traveled from society to society and, as Elder Seth Wells reported, "arrived unexpectedly and inspected in detail what everyone was doing."[39] She died in February 1821 at Watervliet, and is buried there.

After twelve years, the South Family was released in 1822 from temporal and spiritual connection with the Second Family to manage its own affairs under Elder Calvin Wells, Eldress Elizabeth Youngs, and, as assistants, Elder Ezekial Copley and Eldress Ann

Bowser. In June 1823, they moved into a brick dwelling house erected the previous year and executed their own covenant.

Donald MacDonald, traveling with the Scotch socialist and philanthropist Robert Owen in 1824, went to see the Shakers with a letter of introduction from Governor Clinton. The visitors were favorably impressed with the industry displayed in the workshops by carpenters, joiners, whip makers, coopers, shoemakers, and tailors. They were shown silver pens and clay pipes made by Shaker craftsmen, and a "Piggery with some of the finest swine we had ever seen." In a small, neat room, they were seated at a clean table to partake of a meal consisting of "beefsteaks, boiled beef, pork and vegetables, sweets, apples, apple tarts, squash, salt bread, good cheese and butter and excellent cider."[40] (Perhaps the introduction from the governor had some influence.) The Shakers explained to them that a man might have a choice of trades, that some members traveled to visit other Shakers at the society's expense, and that no one worked more than he was able or willing to do.

Another well-known visitor from the world, James Fenimore Cooper, in *The Traveling Bachelor* letters of 1824 referred to the Niskayuna Shakers as "an orderly, industrious sect, and models of decency, cleanliness, and of morality." He noted "order and arrangement, without, however, being picturesque or ornamented." Although "in one or two instances, the courts have interpreted the laws as humanely in their favour as circumstances would reasonably allow," he concludes "there is no fear that this, or any other religious sect that is founded altogether on fanaticism and folly, will ever arrive to the smallest importance."[41]

From 1794 to 1826 the Shakers' property was augmented by 400 acres once belonging to Benjamin Youngs and deeded to them a piece at a time by Youngs or his heirs (Youngs already had a family when he became a Shaker). By 1825 they had also acquired William Carter's land, where Memory's Gardens, a private cemetery, is today. The 1825 census records of the Shakers at Niskayuna show that 89.9 of their acres were improved. Additional Niskayuna statistics include 4 heads of families, 112 males, 153 females (29 under sixteen, 73 aged sixteen to forty-five, and 51 over forty-five), 155 head of cattle, 22 horses, 475 sheep, and 134 hogs. The community is credited with 1,450 yards of fulled cloth, 1,945 yards of flannel, and 4,464 yards of linen and cotton made in one year.

Perhaps Thomas Jefferson was referring to the Shakers, when he wrote in 1822 that, "on the principle of a communion of property, small societies may exist in habits of virtue, order, industry, and peace, and consequently in a state of as much happiness as Heaven has been pleased to deal out to imperfect humanity."[42] The catalogue of the Library of Congress lists Thomas Brown's book, *An Account of the People Called Shakers,* in Thomas Jefferson's personal library.

General view of Church Family buildings as they appeared in 1927. (New York State History Collection)

South Family dwelling (or bell) house. For many years it has been common belief that this residence was built in 1822, but newly discovered material from the South Family records, substantiated by the writings of Thomas Brown, strengthens the theory that this is the dwelling house built in 1800 for the young Believers. The bell and one-story extension were added in 1848. (New York State History Collection)

These measured architectural drawings show the South Family dwelling house with original details based on information from Eldress Anna Case, who lived there from 1866 to 1938. The cross section shows the doors used as a folding partition in the original meeting room on the first floor. This same building was described by Thomas Brown in 1812 as "a large commodious house," in the lower part of which a partition opened and enlarged the meeting room. (Library of Congress, Historic American Buildings Survey)

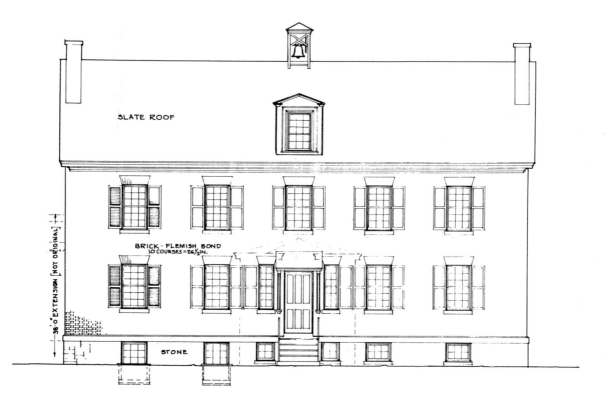

SLATE ROOF

BRICK · FLEMISH BOND
10 COURSES = 26½ IN.

STONE

38'-0 EXTENSION [NOT ORIGINAL]

The little frame cottage considered the earliest South Family building, though referred to as the original home, could not possibly have housed the approximately sixteen young Believers who constituted the family in 1800. This cottage was later known as the sauce and jelly house, and before it was razed (after 1939) it was used for scalding pigs. (New York State History Collection)

Although Thomas Brown differed with the theology of the Shakers, he left us with a favorable impression of their advance in building at the close of the 1790s: "I am not of the opinion of many, that they will soon become extinct. . . . See their whole attenuated force collected under the roof of a log-hut, surrounded with the towering pines . . . and then behold the present contrast! See the once uncultivated wilderness waste of Niskeuna and other places, now turned into fruitful fields — see their neat public edifices towering amidst the surrounding elegance and neatness of their more private habitations."

Above: *Church Family dwelling house (second house), built 1790, as it appeared shortly before demolition in 1927. (New York State History Collection)*

Right: *Church Family ministry house, built 1825, as it appeared in 1927. (New York State History Collection)*

By the turn of the century the Church Family had recorded a total of thirteen buildings.

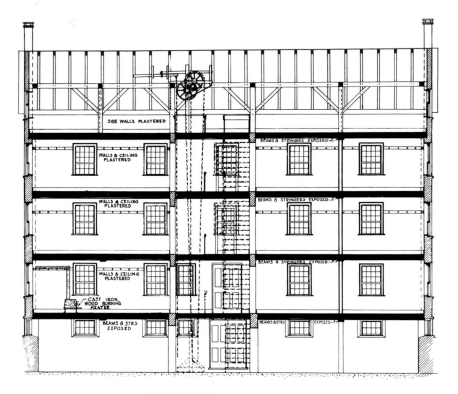

The South Family records show that it had outgrown the rest of the society in 1810, and that another dwelling house was built to accommodate a newly organized West Family of young Believers. It is very likely that this is the 1810 dwelling house. It was converted to a workshop when the present bell house was erected in 1828. (National Gallery of Art, Index of American Design)

SIDE WALLS PLASTERED

WALLS & CEILING PLASTERED

BEAMS & STRINGERS EXPOSED

WALLS & CEILING PLASTERED

BEAMS & STRINGERS EXPOSED

WALLS & CEILING PLASTERED

BEAMS & STRINGERS EXPOSED

CAST IRON WOOD BURNING HEATER

BEAMS & STRS EXPOSED

BEAMS & STRS EXPOSED

LONGITUDINAL   SECTION

This twentieth-century section of the West Family's 1810 building indicates that one of the original staircases could have been removed to install the hoist used in the workshop. (Library of Congress, Historic American Buildings Survey)

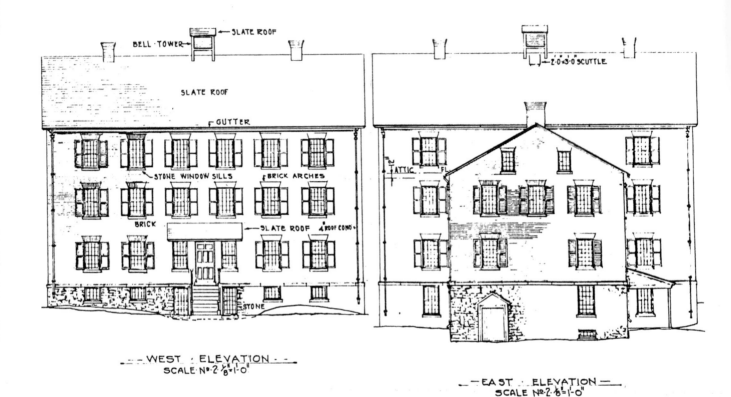

WEST · ELEVATION
SCALE Nº 2 ⅛"=1'-0"

EAST · ELEVATION
SCALE Nº 2 ⅛"=1'-0"

The West Family dwelling house, or bell house, has always been assigned 1828 as the date of construction because of a painted tin strip bearing the date, located on the upper floor over the stairs. (Reproduced courtesy of Francis Spoonogle)

These twentieth-century architectural drawings of the West Family's 1828 building show the west facade as originally constructed, without a porch, but include the rear wing added in 1887. (Library of Congress, Historic American Buildings Survey)

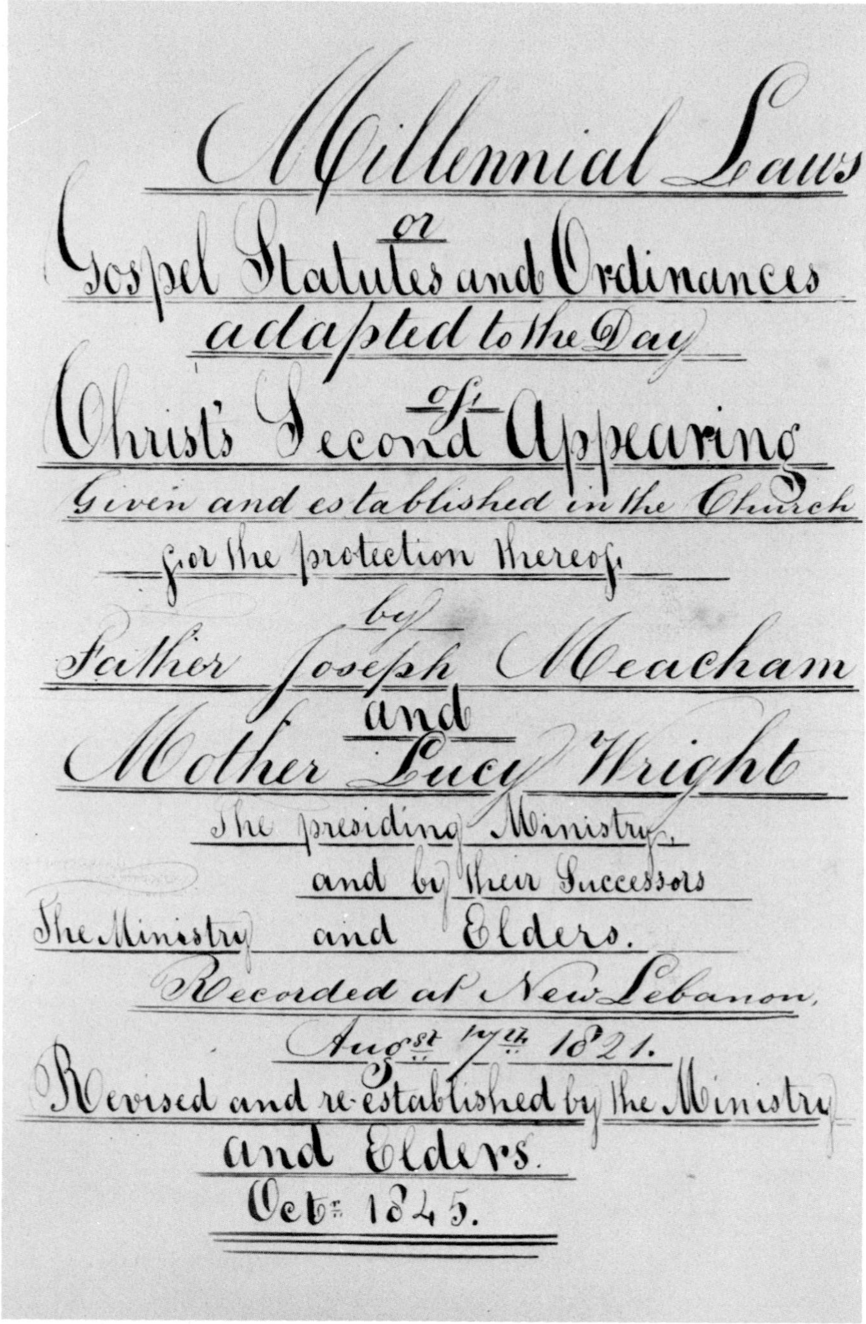

Since there was rarely more than one copy of the Millennial Laws in each family in any of the Shaker communities, it is understandable that this is the only one which has been located from Watervliet. This is a copy of the 1845 revision of the original Statutes and Ordinances set forth in 1821 by Father Joseph Meacham and Mother Lucy Wright. (New York State Library Collection)

Millennial Laws

or

Gospel Statutes and Ordinances adapted to the Day of Christ's Second Appearing

Given and established in the Church for the protection thereof.

by

Father Joseph Meacham and Mother Lucy Wright

The presiding Ministry, and by their Successors

The Ministry and Elders.

Recorded at New Lebanon,

Augst 17th 1821.

Revised and re-established by the Ministry and Elders.

Octr 1845.

Far left: Nineteenth-century Shaker suit. The butternut worsted coat and trousers and the blue vest depicted were characterized as "winter best" by Faith and Edward Andrews. **Left:** *Nineteenth-century Shaker dress. Butternut dye was used for this dress as well as the man's suit. The kerchief is described as being made of rose silk. (National Gallery of Art, Index of American Design)*

The earliest documentation of the appearance of the Shakers is either in descriptions or drawings of their dancing during worship. In 1817, the French author and illustrator J. Milbert described their dress with an artist's eye for detail:

"The women wore mantles of fine fabric over deep-violet silk sheaths, fichus of immaculate white linen, elbow-length gray gloves, and satin bonnets with projecting brims and a flat pleated back. The mens' clothing was also uniform and very neat. It consisted of a grayish-white coat with a broad waist and large tails, a long vest containing pockets, and short trousers tied with ribbons. They wore yellow-topped boots and a broad-brimmed round hat with a small crown. . . . Their pale, thin faces, most of them [the women] far from pretty, betokened their very austere life."

*Shakers dancing the Square Order Shuffle.
Notice the contrast between the top hat and
cane at the right or the costume of the visitor
seated on the left and the wide-brimmed hats
on the pegboards or the plain gowns,
kerchiefs, and caps of the Shaker sisters. The
napkins over the sisters' arms were probably
used to "mop the brow" after the strenuous
dancing. The waistcoated brethren (both
black and white) have removed their coats
and tied up their sleeves.*

Top: *Shaker school. Little attention had been paid to education at Watervliet before 1818, but in 1823 the brick school shown at right was built on the Church Family property because of the interest of Mother Lucy Wright. Donald MacDonald mentions seeing a copy of* Lindley Murray's Exercises *at this schoolhouse in 1824 and notes that garden seeds, "their principle object of traffic," were kept on the second floor. Seth Y. Wells was in charge, but as an officially designated free school system (School District No. 14) the school was ultimately under the jurisdiction of the town of Watervliet inspectors. Initially, there were female students in the summer and male in the winter (probably because in summer all male hands were needed in the fields), but by the early 1900s boys and girls classes were held together. After this school was closed, classes were held at the South Family school until 1926. The 1823 Church Family school building was demolished in 1926. The Ann Lee Home power station was built on its foundation. (New York State History Collection)*

Bottom: *Church Family brick shop, built 1822. The date stone in the basement of this building reads "Bruster and Allen, master masons." The building was remodeled to serve as the nurses residence of the Ann Lee Home. (New York State History Collection)*

From the old South Family records we know that there were two dwelling houses built at the South Family, one in 1800 and a second in 1822. The building shown at right is more logically the 1822 house: there is no interior evidence of a folding partition that Thomas Brown observed in a South Family dwelling in 1812, and the brick basements observable in this photograph were not common in the Albany area until after 1800. A photograph of the building labeled old community house in a Shaker scrapbook at Sabbathday Lake identifies it as having once been used as a communal dwelling. The Index of American Design files indicate that it was also used as a trustees' office and a cannery. (National Gallery of Art, Index of American Design)

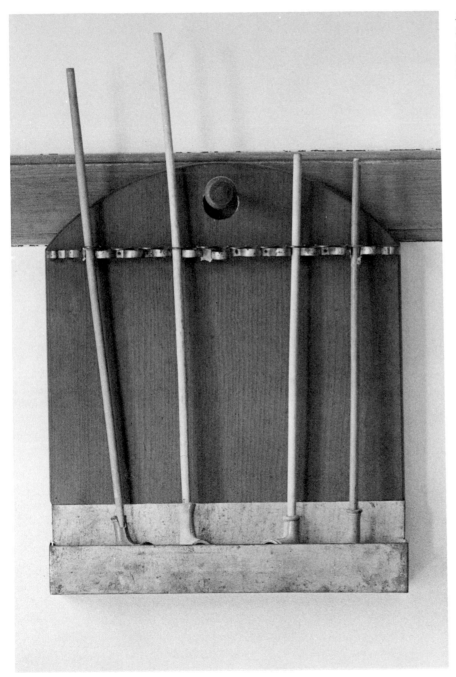

Pipe making was a Watervliet industry in the early 1800s, and the rack as well as the white- and red-bowled pipes shown here are Watervliet products. (Hancock Shaker Village)

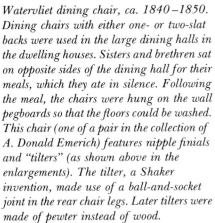*Watervliet dining chair, ca. 1840–1850. Dining chairs with either one- or two-slat backs were used in the large dining halls in the dwelling houses. Sisters and brethren sat on opposite sides of the dining hall for their meals, which they ate in silence. Following the meal, the chairs were hung on the wall pegboards so that the floors could be washed. This chair (one of a pair in the collection of A. Donald Emerich) features nipple finials and "tilters" (as shown above in the enlargements). The tilter, a Shaker invention, made use of a ball-and-socket joint in the rear chair legs. Later tilters were made of pewter instead of wood.*

Right: *Tall chest, ca. 1810.*

Unlike the Mt. Lebanon Shaker community which ran an extensive chair industry, the Watervliet Shakers did not make furniture to sell to the world. However, they did make a quantity of different types of chests, tables, and beds for their own use.

Above: *Mirror rack, ca. 1820.*

Far left: *Tall narrow cupboard, ca. 1810.*

Left: *Counter, ca. 1820.*

A Golden Crown of Comfort and Rest from heavy sufferings

Given by Father William to Elder Brother Bishop.

48

1825–1850

The peak of population was reached at the Watervliet Shaker community somewhere in the period between 1825 and 1850, climbing from 200 and possibly reaching 350. Official United States census records show 304 in 1840. A Shaker census taken in 1844 gives a total of 326 individuals. Between 1845 and 1850 the population may have risen from 326 to 350. The latter figure is given by Charles Nordhoff, who collected his information directly from the Shakers in 1875, and it should be given some credence although the official 1850 U.S. census figure is only 278.

For the first time the census of 1830 listed the Niskayuna Shaker population as being Shakers under four heads of families; no out families were included. The total had risen to 246. The figures included two blacks and twenty aliens. The family of Samuel Pease (Church) is given 87 members; that of David Hawkin[g]s (North) 38 members; that of Stephen Wells (West) 60 members; and that of Calvin Wells (South) 61 members. It is from the non-Shaker census enumerator that we learn about the black members. The Shakers themselves did not usually differentiate.

This was a period when the world visited the Shakers. Governors, legislators, foreign diplomats, and authors came, and so did plain curiosity-seekers. It was also a period of divine inspiration (called Mother's Work by the Shakers). Communications were received from the spirit world, and spiritual names were given to Shaker communities. Watervliet became Wisdom's Valley. Shaker industry flourished and inventions were numerous. Shakers made or raised nearly everything needed for their own use, and as time progressed, some of their products were sold to the world

Phebe Smith received and recorded a visionary message from James Wardley, Jr., the deceased son of James and Jane Wardley, the founders of Shakerism in England, at Watervliet in 1839. In 1846 Sister Phebe converted the message into a spirit drawing, titled "A Golden Crown of Comfort and Rest from heavy Sufferings." (Western Reserve Historical Society Collection)

and even developed as major industries. At Watervliet, the latter included bonnets, fine shirts, and flat brooms. A medicinal herb business was also extensive. A garden seed business, which had a modest beginning at Watervliet in the 1790s, gradually increased in volume under the administration of David Osborne.

The daily family diaries record constant construction, moving, and remodeling of buildings, at both Church and South Families. At the latter, in 1827 a four-story frame building, forty by sixty feet, was erected west of the second house for a sisters' shop and wash and engine room, and again in 1829 a three-story brick shop, sixty-two by forty-two feet, was finished — this one for the brethren.

The covenant of the young Believers order (South Family), originally signed in 1823, was rewritten in 1830. The new covenant, to which names were added up to 1912, was to be "a witness for the family in order to secure to ourselves our just and natural right and privileges according to the laws of God and the free institution of our country and prevent collisions and litigations and insure justice and equity to our fellow creatures as far as depends on our connections and intercourse with them."[43]

Random entries from the South Family records give great and small insight into life in this period. An 1832 entry about jailing for "non-performance of militia service" notes that although "application was made by many respectable inhabitants of Albany for execution of clemency; the Brethren remained in close confinement in the putrid air of the common deposit of evil doers, the full period of fourteen days." In 1844 Hannah Youngs, "a Covenant member, removes to the 2nd F" [and] "wills her Eight-day clock to the Elders of the S.F."; and in 1848 "we put up a bell on the dwelling house, which weighs 227 lbs. & cost $76.10," and "we abandon the use of pork, and sell off our hogs & pork."

Some are more momentous. On 11 May 1835,

"Joseph P. goes to Lebanon & the Brethren dig up first Mother & Father Williams graves and a young man. Great many of our Brethren and Sisters goes to the grave to see them. The out Families has liberty to come and see the bones." On 12 May "they bury the bones in the burying yard. They move Mother Lucy grave a little."[44]

A marginal note on the 1839 "Plan of Watervliet, N.Y." explains the disinterment, stating that the site of Mother Ann's first grave did not belong to the Believers. The "young man" referred to in the 11 May entry was William Bigsby, who traveled to Niskayuna to observe the new religion, became ill, died, and was buried there in 1781. His remains were removed to the present cemetery along with those of Mother Ann and Father William Lee. The note on the map strengthens the supposition that they were first buried on the original tract the Believers leased in 1775. At the time of Mother Ann's death, they still leased the tract, but had moved the center of activities to the site of the present Church Family. We know that Richard Hocknell (then a married backslider) obtained a lease for the tract from Van Rensselaer in 1788, but can find no explanation for why the Believers waited until 1835 to move Mother Ann.

The Shakers continued to be of interest to the world, and visitors increased in number and importance. Alexis de Tocqueville and Gustave de Beaumont visited the Niskayuna Shakers in 1831, and Tocqueville wrote of a Shaker dance: "They placed themselves two by two in a curving line . . . held their elbows against the body, stretched out their forearms and let their hands hang, which gave them the air of trained dogs who are forced to walk on their hind legs." The Catholic Tocqueville added that "we had with us a young American Protestant, who said to us on leaving: 'two more spectacles like that, and I become a Catholic.'"[45]

Herman Melville's *Moby Dick* tells of a member of the crew of the *Jeroboam* having been "nurtured among the crazy society of the Neskeuna Shakers, where he had been a great prophet; in their cracked, secret meetings, having several times descended from heaven by the way of a trap-door."[46] Melville, who lived in Albany from 1830 until 1838 and wrote some of his first books in Lansingburgh, north of Troy, in 1838, must have had firsthand knowledge of the Niskayuna Shakers.

A more complimentary, anonymous description was reprinted from the *Boston Palladium* by the *Niles Weekly Register* in 1829: "It is impossible," the writer notes, "to describe the air of tranquility and comfort that diffuses itself over a Shaker settlement . . . the two sexes together bear the burden, if burden it may be, of celibacy. . . . The union of these people, their uniform kindness to each other, and the singularly benevolent and tender expression of their countenances, speak a stronger language than their professions."[47]

Elias Raub, a teacher from Troy, left impressions of an 1837 Sunday meeting. To him the sisters, child and adult alike, "presented a very singular appearance, looking like so many corpses, all dressed in white and looking as pale as death." He quotes a Believer as telling the visitors that "we are no longer the people of the world, but the children of God. We have left the world and all its follies, vices and passions." Later came the dancing, described by Raub as a "complete hoe down" which "set many of the Worldly people laughing, to which the Shakers, very justly, made many long faces." Even though Raub subdued his own laughter, he believed that the Shakers were a happy people and would have many more converts if "intermarriage was not prohibited among them."[48]

The celebrated actress Charlotte Cushman visited in 1837, as did J. Silk Buckingham, a British traveler. The latter noted that "the greater number [of women] were very plain . . . with an appearance of langor, that betokened a morbid state of feeling, and very imperfect health," commented on the singing as "loud and harsh without the least attempt at harmony," and described the dancing of the "more robust" as literally leaping to the tune of "Nancy Dawson," a popular song among sailors during his own youth in England. "During the whole period," he concluded, "I was endeavoring to settle in my mind the debatable question . . . were they practicing a delusion on themselves or endeavoring to impose upon and deceive others."[49] He concluded that instead of others they were deluding themselves.

Shaker diaries are usually anonymous, but one particularly charming 1837–50 Church Family journal is known to be the work of Sister Ann Buckingham — a member of a large family, most of whom joined the Watervliet Shakers in their teens, lived long, productive lives, and died in the faith. Seven Buckinghams are buried at Watervliet including David Austin Buckingham, the historian and teacher. From Sister Ann we learn about visitors who came by invitation — Gov. William L. Marcy and Mrs. Marcy; groups of legislators; a small group of black Philadelphia Shaker sisters (organized by Sister Rebecca Jackson of Watervliet); others from the Groveland ministry and the Ohio ministry (to learn how to make cheese); and brethren from New Lebanon (to help raise the mill).

In 1837 she notes of a death that a sister "took her flight to the world of spirits," and of whitewashing meeting rooms, "clean is the theme." Her records for 1843 inform us that "about 300 silk worms have hatched out," later that "silkworms have begun to wind the second time," and still later that "Moriah T. & myself went to reeling silk." In 1846 she writes that "young sisters [are] making garden seed bags," and "the bluebirds begin to sing." In December of the same year she tells us of walnut "timber for meeting house [benches], which came from Groveland," the next year that they "raise new meetinghouse" and "the families all eat in the new kitchen — 101 bros. sit down together."[50]

In 1839 the New York State legislature passed an act which validated all trust instruments conveying property to the Shakers before 1830, but held that any such transaction after 1830 would be limited to trusts providing an annual income of no more than $5,000. The fact that trustees could legally hold such property for the society was probably an important factor in the reframing of the South Family covenant in 1830. Samuel J. Tilden, who was very active in the legislation for limiting Shaker trusts, wrote in 1839 of Shaker opposition that they wanted "to have their property exempted from the operation of the general laws of the State applicable to trusts."[51]

In 1849 the act concerning Shaker trusts was amended to allow ownership to descend in regular succession from trustee to trustee without executing further documents. By 1852 the limitation on the annual income of property in trust was increased from $5,000 to $25,000. It is interesting to note that finally this figure was amended to $2 million.

In 1872 a writer who called herself Daughtie published her account of "Fifteen Years A Shakeress at Wisdom's Valley" in *The Galaxy*. She had left the Shakers for the world some time previously, but her impressions trace back to the 1840s. There are poignant memories — children being told to pinch their cheeks for color to dispel the rumors that they were pale, unhealthy, and kept against their will, and that although not allowed any dolls, she was "rebellious, and often made a corn-cob wrapped in a bit of muslin; with a chestnut-shell cap on the smaller end." Daughtie's "caretaker" indulged in small cruelties — "cold hands down her back" or "scissors pressed into her hand," neither as insufferable as being made to wear a frilled, "world" nightcap (to Daughtie, a "crown of thorns"). The one remembered case of real cruelty, the beating of some of the boys, resulted in a brother's being exiled to another community.

Daughtie's vivid account discloses the humiliation of those begging to return to the Shakers after going to the world; the public rebuke of a brother who failed to seek the elders' permission for a trip to New York City; and a sister's having to read aloud her love letters from one of the brethren. She left for the world, however, "with a tender memory of my childhood's home."[52]

It was in the 1840s that spiritual names were given to the Shaker communities, and the village first known as Niskayuna, then Watervliet, became known as Wisdom's Valley. Daughtie mentions extraordinary communications were being received from the spirit world during her childhood, with whirling, spinning, and speaking in strange tongues, and that "the lively spirits were delightful to us children." This was an expression of the divine inspiration of Shakerism from 1837 to 1852. Legend tells us that an angelic vision was seen by two young girls at Watervliet in 1837 and that more and more Shakers subsequently experienced divinely inspired visions.

A vision of Brother Philemon Stewart of New Lebanon revealed that each Shaker community should set apart a piece of ground for outdoor worship. During the years 1842 and 1843 the societies established their feast grounds, or worship areas, with large fountain stones (large slab monuments with lengthy incised inscriptions) at the center. The outdoor ceremonies were held principally in May and September for about a decade, when a message was again received to "take care of them."[53] Most of these stones then vanished or were destroyed in an attempt to hide the exact locations of the feast grounds.

Shaker historians say that the two most important books about the period of spiritualism were written by Brother Philemon Stewart and Sister Paulina Bates. Sister Paulina received a vision on 1 September 1842 that the book would be written by divine inspiration through the instrument of a member of the Second Family at Wisdom's Valley. The elders testified that "we immediately furnished a room in the most still and retired part of the dwelling house for her accommodation to resort to whenever she was summoned by the trumpet of the Holy Angel to receive the word of God." The resulting work, *The Divine Book of Holy and Eternal Wisdom*, was published at Canterbury, New Hampshire, in 1849. Elders Seth Y. Wells and Calvin Green appear as editors, and "Jesus Christ, Ann Lee, King Solomon, and the Archangel of Love" as witnesses to Sister Paulina's inspiration.[54]

Some visions were expressed in the form of spirit drawings. One such was "Narrative of James Wardley, Jr., Seen and wrote down in Vision by Phebe Ann Smith of Watervliet, March 4th, 1839."[55]

Periodically, the interest of the world became a nuisance, and the Shakers would post on the Great Gate of Wisdom's Valley notices like that of 22 October 1847, which declares that "we hereby notify who may resort to this place of worship on the Sabbath that public meetings are again discontinued," and concludes that "we would take it as a great favor (to all who have hitherto enjoyed) if gunners would also cease from annoying us on the Sabbath with their shooting, for it is very offensive to our feelings."[56]

Joel Munsell must have known the Shakers himself to have written in his *Annals of Albany* in 1850, "Though for a long time distinguished by gross ignorance and superstition, they are now feeling, slowly, the influence of the intelligence of the times, bestow some attention on letters, and mingle somewhat more freely . . . with the world."[57]

The sisters at Watervliet carried on a good business of bonnet making with diary entries showing "six dozen sold to a New York City man" in 1837; "Elizabeth Seely has made 18 bonnets for home use" in 1845; and, in 1851, "Clarissa and Lydia packed bonnets for Harvard — four boxes at $172 worth." A daybook recording the sale of bonnets spans two decades — 1836–1856. Early bonnets were made of straw, later ones of palm leaves — an art perfected by the New York sisters. (National Gallery of Art, Index of American Design)

Top: *Herb cutter. (New York State History Collection)*

Bottom: *Herb press. (New York State History Collection)*

Left: *Herb label printing press. (New York State History Collection)*

54

The herb industry at Watervliet was considerable. Over 1,827 items were advertised in catalogues, the first of which was published for the Shakers in Albany in 1830 and asked the question, "Why send to Europe's distant shores/ For plants which grow at our doors?" The Shakers printed their own labels but also purchased from the world, as shown by the bill in 1838 for 16,500 labels at a cost of ten dollars. One entry in a sister's diary of 22 August 1837 says, "Collect 300 lbs. of lobelia." Lobelia was a medicinal herb used as a respiratory stimulant.

Top right: *Packaged herbs. "Inspissated" means thickened. (New York State History Collection)*

Bottom right: *Bill for herb labels. (Western Reserve Historical Society Collection)*

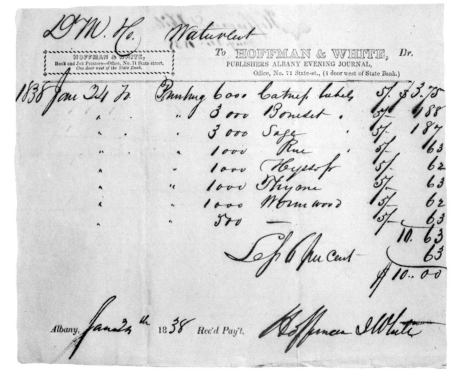

Sewing cabinet. Though in this period furniture was made by other Shaker communities for sale to the world, this sewing cabinet was probably made in Watervliet for the use of a Watervliet sister. It is attributed to Freegift Wells, who appears in the 1850 census as a joiner, aged 65. (New York State History Collection)

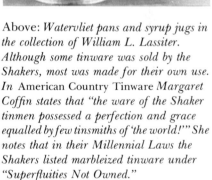

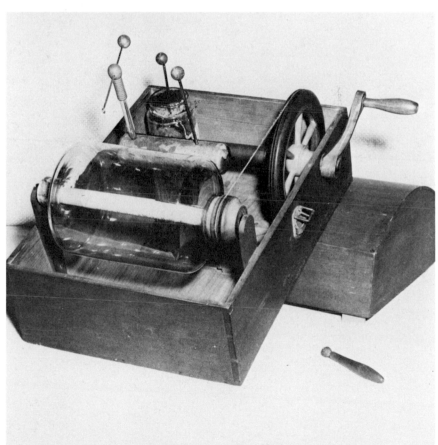

Circular saw blade. The invention of the circular saw is attrbuted to the Watervliet Shakers in a Niles Weekly Register *of 1821 which stated that the Shakers felt this invention was of such great importance that the right to reproduce it should belong to the world and that they would not seek to patent it. (New York State History Collection)*

Above: *Watervliet pans and syrup jugs in the collection of William L. Lassiter. Although some tinware was sold by the Shakers, most was made for their own use. In* American Country Tinware *Margaret Coffin states that "the ware of the Shaker tinmen possessed a perfection and grace equalled by few tinsmiths of 'the world!'" She notes that in their Millennial Laws the Shakers listed marbleized tinware under "Superfluities Not Owned."*

Right: *Electrostatic machine, marked F. S. Wicker, 1822. This model, perfected for therapeutic treatment by Frederick S. Wicker of Watervliet, was almost certainly based on a similar one made by Brother Thomas Corbett of Canterbury, ca. 1810. Static electricity made by the contact of a piece of silk with the revolving cylinder was stored in the glass jar. The electricity was then applied to the patient's body by electrodes. (New York State History Collection)*

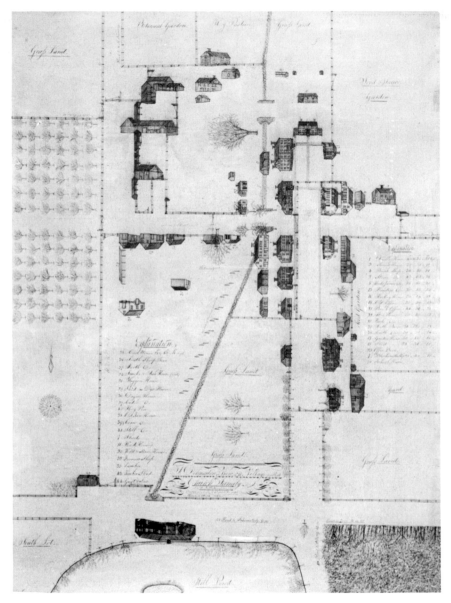

Right: *Walnut benches of the Church Family new meetinghouse were installed in 1847. We know that there was a walnut grove at the Groveland community near Rochester, and Sister Ann Buckingham's diary for 21 December 1846 notes that "Brothers turn out 9 teams to Schenectady after timber for meetinghouse, which came from Groveland." (Emma B. King Library, Shaker Museum, Old Chatham.)*

Left: *"A Delineation or View of the Village called the Church Family" by David Austin Buckingham, 1838, is drawn to scale, and with its legends giving measurements, has aided in location of some original buildings which would not otherwise have been identified. The "Old Office No. 18," which appears to be a smaller replica of the 1791 meetinghouse, stands on the site where the second meetinghouse was built in 1847. There is no record of when the old office was built or razed. Brother David Austin Buckingham was a teacher, cartographer, tailor, gardener, postmaster, and a reliable Shaker historian. A member of the large natural family of Buckinghams, he was many years a Shaker and is buried in the Watervliet cemetery. (New York State History Collection)*

Church Family old and new meetinghouses, 1791 and 1847. Only the old meetinghouse appears in Buckingham's 1838 view, of course. The new meetinghouse (at right) measured 54' x 113' and was of frame construction. It has been refaced with brick, still stands, and is used as the Catholic chapel of Saint Elizabeth's of Hungary. There is some discrepancy about the actual date of the original construction. Although there was some possible construction during 1846 (the date commonly assigned to the building of the second meetinghouse), Sister Ann Buckingham's diary entry of 18 February 1847 notes that "we have the gift to go ahead and build a new meetinghouse" and, on 27 June 1847: "Raise new meetinghouse. Oliver Prentice's boys, all the brethren in the Society that could do as much as pull a rope, came to the raising." (New York State History Collection)

Bought of CHAUNCY MILLER.

☞ No Seed Warranted, and no damages allowed above the price of the Seeds when sold.

POUNDS		DOLLS.	CTS.
	ASPARAGUS ...Giant,		
	BEET ......Early Blood Turnip,		
	do ......Early Bassona,		
	do ......Egyptian Turnip,		
	do ......Long Blood,		
	do ......Yellow Sugar,		
	do ......White Sugar,		
	do ......Long Red Mangel Wurtzel,		
	do ......Yellow Globe Mangel Wurtzel,		
BUSHELS	BEANS ......Early China,		
	do ......Early Mohawk,		
	do ......Early Six Weeks, long,		
	do ......Early Six Weeks, round,		
	do ......Early Rachel,		
	do ......Refugees, or Thousand to One,		
	do ......Early Butter, Black or Wax,		
	do ......Early White Butter,		
	do ......Horticultural, or Speckled Cranberry,		
	do ......White Runners,		
	do ......Large Lima,		
POUNDS	CABBAGE ......Early York,		
	do ......Early Ox Heart, English,		
	do ......Early Ox Heart, French,		
	do ......Early Wakefield, American,		
	do ......Fottler's Improved Brunswick,		
	do ......Early Winningstadt,		
	do ......Green Globe Savoy,		
	do ......Drumhead Winter,		
	do ......Premium Flat Dutch,		
	do ......Marblehead Mammoth,		
	do ......Large Bristol,		
	do ......Red Dutch,		
	CAULIFLOWER Early London,		
	do ......Early Paris,		
	do ......Early Dwarf Erfurt,		
	do ......Lenormands,		
	do ......Walcheven,		
	CARROT ......Early Horn,		
	do ......Long Orange,		
	do ......Long White,		
	CELERY ......White Solid,		
BUSHELS	CORN ......Extra Early,		
	do ......Bates' Extra Early,		
	do ......Crosby's Early,		
	do ......Large Twelve Rowed,		
	do ......Stowell's Evergreen,		
POUNDS	CUCUMBER ...Early Russian,		
	do ......Early Frame,		
	do ......Early Cluster,		
	do ......Long Green,		
	do ......White Spined,		
	CRESS ......Double Pepper Grass,		
	EGGPLANT ...Purple,		
	KOHLRABI ...Large Green,		
	LEEK,		
	LETTUCE ......Early Boston Curled,		
	do ......Early Curled Silesia,		
	do ......Large Cabbage Head,		
	do ......Frankford Head,		
	do ......India Cape,		
	MARJORAM ...Sweet,		
	MELON ......Early Christiana,		
	do ......Green Fleshed Nutmeg,		
	Amount carried forward ...... $		

POUNDS		DOLLS.	CTS.
	Amount brought forward		
	MELON ......Rough Skin Musk,		
	do ......Mountain Sweet,		
	do ......Black Spanish,		
	do ......Citron (for preserves),		
	ONION ......White,		
POUNDS	do ......Red,		
	do ......Yellow Danvers,		
	do ......Yellow Dutch,		
BUSHELS	do ......Onion Sets, White,		
	do ......Onion Sets, Yellow,		
	do ......Potato Onions,		
POUNDS	PARSLEY ......Curled,		
	PARSNEP ......Long Sweet,		
BUSHELS	PEAS ......Carter's First Crop,		
	do ......Caractacus,		
	do ......Early Daniel O'Rourke,		
	do ......Early Dwarf, or Tom Thumb,		
	do ......McLean's Little Gem,		
	do ......Blue Imperial,		
	do ......Champion of England,		
	do ......White Marrowfat,		
	do ......Black Eyed Marrowfat,		
POUNDS	PEPPER ......Large Bell,		
	do ......Large Squash,		
	do ......Sweet Spanish,		
	do ......Cherry,		
	do ......Cayenne,		
	PUMPKIN ......Connecticut Field,		
	RADISH ......Early Scarlet Turnip,		
	do ......Early White Turnip,		
	do ......Early Olive Shaped,		
	do ......Long Scarlet Short Top,		
	do ......Yellow Summer Turnip,		
	do ......White Spanish,		
	do ......Black Spanish Winter,		
	do ......Scarlet Chinese Winter,		
	SALSIFY ......Vegetable Oyster,		
	SAGE ......Common,		
	SAVORY ......Summer,		
	SPINACH ......Prickley,		
	do ......Round Leaved,		
	do ......Large Flanders,		
	SQUASH ......Summer Golden Crookneck,		
	do ......Summer Golden Bush,		
	do ......Turban,		
	do ......Vegetable Marrow,		
	do ......Hubbard,		
	TOMATO ......Trophy,		
	do ......Large Smooth Red,		
	do ......Keys' Early Red,		
	TURNIP ......White Strap Leaf,		
	do ......Red Strap Leaf,		
	do ......White Flat Dutch,		
	do ......Golden Ball,		
	do ......Sweet Turnip,		
	do ......Ruta Baga,		
	$		

Brother Chauncy Miller (1814–1901), trustee of the Watervliet Church Family. (Western Reserve Historical Society Collection)

Left: *Chauncy Miller's seed list. (New York State History Collection)*

The seed business, which had a modest beginning at Watervliet in the 1790s, gradually increased in volume. In 1811, Morrell Baker perfected the cultivation of seeds to a degree that increased income appreciably — reaching thousands of dollars by 1840. As a trustee, Chauncy Miller was responsible for the sale of seeds to the world.

Patent medicines, distributed throughout the world by mid-nineteenth century, included such Shaker remedies as Laurus Eye Water, manufactured at Watervliet. (New York State Library Collection)

LAURUS EYE WATER.

For the cure of acute and chronic inflammations of the eyes, and morbid weakness of sight.

In diseases of the eye there is an enlargement of its cutaneous vessels, which renders the motions of the eye painful and irritating. This Eye Water contains a delicate mucilage which lubricates the parts; while its tonic properties restore a healthy action.

DIRECTIONS.

Drop some of the water into the eye every four or six hours; and avoid stimulants, intense application and strong light.

Prepared in the United Society, Watervliet, N. Y.

Price 25 cents a bottle, or $2 a dozen.

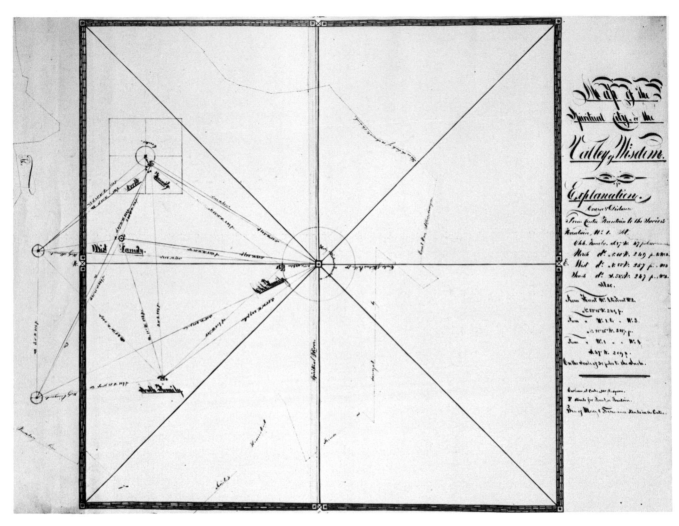

"Map of the Spiritual City of the Valley of Wisdom." Evert Van Alen, a surveyor from Albany County, prepared this map for the Shakers in 1842 showing exactly where the feast grounds and fountain stones — possibly one for each family in Watervliet — were located. (Western Reserve Historical Society Collection)

Using the original survey and map drafted by Van Alen in 1842, this contemporary map was charted to show the exact location of the worship areas.

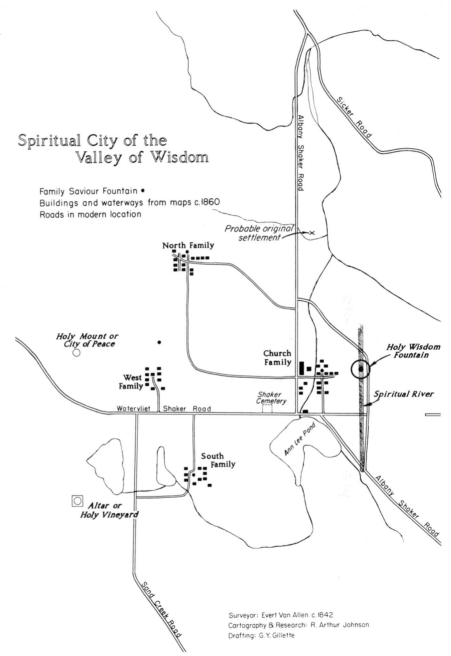

Spiritual City of the Valley of Wisdom

Family Saviour Fountain •
Buildings and waterways from maps c.1860
Roads in modern location

Albany Shaker Road

Sicker Road

Probable original settlement

North Family

Holy Mount or City of Peace

Church Family

Holy Wisdom Fountain

West Family

Shaker Cemetery

Spiritual River

Watervliet Shaker Road

Ann Lee Pond

South Family

Albany Shaker Road

Altar or Holy Vineyard

Sand Creek Road

Surveyor: Evert Van Allen c.1842
Cartography & Research: R. Arthur Johnson
Drafting: G.Y. Gillette

Right: *Spirit drawing, Watervliet, 28 April 1845 (detail). The identity of the Watervliet Shaker who sent the letter containing this spirit drawing to Molly Smith at Hancock in 1847 is unknown. The drawing documents a spirit of communication sent in 1845 to Molly Smith by Isreal Hammond, who had died six years before. (Library of The United Society of Shakers, Sabbathday Lake, Maine)*

Above: *"Narrative of James Wardley, Jr., Seen and wrote down in Vision by Phebe Ann Smith of Watervliet, March 4th, 1839." Benjamin S. Youngs copied the narrative into this hymnal in 1851. (Collection of John Shea)*

Visited by spiritual manifestations in 1830, Rebecca Jackson traveled throughout many states spreading the gospel of her own church before she converted to the Shaker faith. By 1838 she had become the leader of a small group of black Philadelphia Shakers who worked as domestics. Her daughter, Rebecca Jackson Perot, is buried in the Watervliet Shaker cemetery. The "Memoirs of Rebecca Jackson," written by A. G. Hollister of Mt. Lebanon in 1877, are located in the Library of Congress. (Western Reserve Historical Society Collection)

Top: *Watervliet tripod candlestand, ca. 1840.*

Bottom: *Watervliet swivel chair, ca. 1850.*

Left: *Watervliet hymnal cupboard, ca. 1840.*

Shaker dance, from David Lamson's Two
Years Experience Among the Shakers,
*1848. This woodcut depicts the sacred
whirling which is said to have induced the
gift of prophecy when the dancer fell into a
trance.*

MOHAWK

SCHENECTADY CO.

R.S.Pearse
V.Van Vranken
J.McLamarar
W.K.Carney
H.Strong
J.Donnick
H.Strong J.G.
Shakers
HR.Lansing
A.Philips
Store
Mrs.Ireland
Talbott
A.P.
H.L.Whitbeck
P.Oliver
M.Fort
F.I.Onderdonk
A.H.Van Vranken
G.I.Vande
J.H.V.
P.Whitbeck
Shakers
Broom Sh.
J.H.Dunsbach
Tin Sh.
Shakers
S.Conway
H.L.W.
M.M.Fort
M.Dunsbach
J.Groat
J.T.Oliver
Shakers
S.Craigier Sam.Craigier
P.Fero
Brook
G.Freely
E.Link
Mrs.Lank
A.Best
J.W.Miller
Shakers
Morris Hotel
WATERVLIET CENTER
P. O.
A.Groat
M.Foley
D.B.Green
H.C.Raden
G.Hill
S.H.No.1
S.H.Pitts
J.Pollock
H.J.Runkle
B.Pollock
H.Runkle
D.R.Ch.
J.W.Miller
T.Van Volkenburgh
S.M.Cleary
W.Fort
S.Weatherwax
E.R.
A.Siver
L.Sickler
Town
S.Pepper
W.H.Terry
S.Weatherwax
J.Weatherwax
J.Thompson
E.Roff
S.Storm
Wm.Farlee
M.Nedder
G.I.Van Vranken
J.Carpenter
J.B.Pitts
North Family
S.Weatherwax
A.N.Baker
Machine Sh.
B.S.Sh.
Shakers
Wm.Tenbroek
G.Van Olinda
C.Roff
Dwelling
J.Swadland
Wm.Orlop
Dr.J.Wade
Cem.
Machine Sh.
SHAKERS
Shakers
K.Ireland
C.Orlop
Dr.M.Wade
J.Woodbeck
M.Johnson
M.Johnson
G.Marks
Dwelling
Parsonage
M.E.Ch.
H.Coben
L.J.Coben
J.T.I.
West Family
Office
Cem.
Church Family
Hospital
Dwelling
Store
Church
Office
Cem.
J.Becker
A.D.Clute
F.Kunkers
G.T.Witbeck
W.G.
C.Plant
M.Flood
G.T.Johnson
C.P.Lansing
G.Marks
N.Cam
Machine Sh.
B.S.Sh.
Dwelling
Mrs.Hill
J.Ames
J.P.Wiswol
Mrs.Hammond
J.Simmons
South Family
Wm.Wiley
J.Burger
D.Miller
D.R.Ch.
TOWN HOUSE COR
H.McDermot
P.Burger
M.Lutia
Hotel
C.H.Witbeck
Parsonage
A.N.L.
J.Hill
B.S.Sh.
H.L.Vandenburgh
G.Marks
A.X.Ladu
S.H.No.17
J.Hill
A.Hermans
Mrs.O.Vandenburgh
Y.Vandenburgh
Shaker Hotel
J.Hanks
J.Henkes
R.Warner
S.Yearsley
C.Wright
W.Sh.
A.F.Elliot
Mrs.Vanderberg
Mrs.Van Vranken
Witbeck
J.Cramer
F.Fonda
P.G.Fort
P.Beck.
D.Wilbeck
Wm.Swatling
M.Young
Wm.Gramce
W.Cramer
J.M.
J.Osterhout
M.Vanderwarker
B.I.Haswell
W.Haswell
B.Harrington
T.Little
A.Miracle
M.O.
A.Ireland
M.Honan
J.P.Niswall
G.S.Case
H.Harrington
M.R.C.C.C.Sheldon
L.Dedick
Ireland
P.Whitbeck Jr.
A.Watennan
H.H.
J.Calutia
J.Rockenstyre
R.Fiddler
E.Bartlett
Mrs.Goodrich
S.P.Pinchbeck
O.Galutia
D.Dunbar
W.Y.D.Williams
Deyo Brs.
W.Tompkins
D.G.
Wm.Oathout
Dilman
I.Haswell
D.Kirker Mrs.Rose
S.Campbell
Mrs.Stewart
D.Goodrich
M.Nutter
J.Wiggin
L.S.Chase
J.Isdel
Wm.Dunbar
Mrs.Anderson
D.Wellington
HomeLawn Hotel
G.Y.
G.Yearsley
A.Miller
R.T.L.Crofts
J.B.Armour
Coleman
Mrs.Wilson
W.Miller
Cathy
G.L.Lansing
Wm.Quiggle
J.Nash
B.Harrington
J.M.N.
V.Nexon
C.Fenton
E.Pitts
Goodrich
Cem.
J.Turner
H.Weitzel
E.Emmery
J.Maxwell
R.Rockingstyre
J.M.Vo.
E.Welch
H.Garvin
S.H.No.1
W.G.
G.Lawson
E.Dayton
A.Karl
Safford
W.Kirk
J.M.Vo.
W.Arthur
P.Mexon
S.O.
Darling
A.Oathout
A.Van Vranken
E.Weswall
Mrs.C.Quinn
J.McCabe
M.Peet
Store2
J.H.No.1
N.Newton
NEW TONVILLE
P. O.
L.Knap
Weaver
W.Carran
J.Ackroyd
T.Ackroyd
T.Storm
Bap.Ch.
G.N.Griffin
J.Gasbeak
Bingham
J.Riley
P.Culeman
Cong.Ch.
Parrat
C.Neas
K.Ireland
W.Gaffers
J.H.
W.Harvy
J.Bentz
W.Nall
P.Sloan
E.Clark
T.Pinee
J.Gaffers
S.Winnie
H.Walters
Cold Spring
A.Goveo
Palmer
H.Newton
J.Chadwick
F.Smith
Mankle
H.Miller
O.Osborne
A.P.
H.R.Remsen
J.Goeway
WEST TROY
P. O.
Lockrow
W.Grounds
W.J.Becker
J.W.R.Armes
Judge Osborne
J.Henry
F.Prime
J.C.Schuyler
C.Bates
J.Wiegand
J.W.R.
A.H.
F.Folk
L.Schuyler Est.
D.Worth
McCann
T.I.ElRoy
M.Mahan
A.Hartman
T.Lanshey
B.S.Sh.
J.Call
Mrs.Kelly
J.Constantine
Shakers
S.McElroy
C.Shaw
P.Kirker
A.McNary
A.Harrington
Hotel
J.McNutt
E.Weaver
T.Johnson
IRELANDS COR
P. O.

TROY

SCHENECTADY

1850–1875

Although both industry and real estate of the Watervliet community continued to increase in this period, population declined steadily. The largest drop occurred during the Civil War: the United States census population of 274 for 1860 (120 males, 154 females) is reduced to 200 in 1870 (97 males, 103 females). The raw census data of 1875 indicate a total population of 166, including at least 22 hired men. Charles Nordhoff recorded 75 hired hands at the same time. Setting the difference aside, it is significant that the Shakers were becoming more dependent on the world to compensate for their decreased male population. Of the total population, about half were either under sixteen or over forty years of age. Even with these members of the community contributing to productivity, it was necessary to depend on hired hands to continue with construction and heavy agricultural activities. At the same time the Great Gate was intermittently closed to the public because of visitors' "disrespectful, not to say irreverant action,"[58] although the Shakers continued to care for the world's children.

Financially, they were prospering. The Albany County Clerk's records reveal that in this period the Shakers invested over $32,000 in additional real estate. The Beers atlas of 1866 points out that "there was a saw mill, grist mill and a broom factory . . . all operated and owned by the Shakers" on the Mohawk River property.[59]

They continued to keep their property in perfect order with committees appointed within families for equal distribution of work and ownership. One such

Map of Watervliet from the Atlas of Albany County, *published by F. W. Beers & Co. in 1866. The Shakers once claimed they could walk across their own land from Shaker Island in the Mohawk River to within a few miles of the city of Albany. On this 1866 map may be seen not only the sawmill on the Shakers' Mohawk River property, but a broom shop as well. Note also Shaker properties at Irelands Corners (now Loudonville).*

committee, appointed in 1851, allowed for hiring of masons and the "rest to be done by ourselves without hiring" and designated which brethren would "milk every Sabbath morning and all other times that the foreman would deem it unsuitable for the sisters to milk."[60] Ownership of real estate was assigned to specific Shaker families. An 1860 document divided titles to over 1,000 acres of land between the First and Second Orders of the Church Family (the latter being the North Family), specifying that "in consideration of the superior quality of the land set off to the second order," the First Order would take title to all land possessed in Illinois and a lot in Virginia "now considered very valuable."[61] Interest in businesses was also divided. The North Family received the broom business, the sweet corn business, the pipe business, and the privilege of raising garden seeds and herbs. The stone quarry went to the North Family, and the claim to the sawmill to the Church Family. All of these industries continued to thrive with hired labor.

One of the many ingenious inventions of the Shakers was a hermetically sealed tin can for vegetables, and a tin factory was maintained on the road to the river islands. Rose water was sold to the world, with over thirty acres used for growing roses at one time. *Frank Leslie's Illustrated Newspaper* of 11 January 1873 states that "in the line of the preparation of vegetable medicines the Shakers have distanced all competition, and are literally masters of the field."[62]

Visitors continued to come on the Sabbath when the Great Gate was open. An entry dated 8 August 1852 estimates that there were 144 carriages, and the following week's entry reports "over 150 carriages at meeting today; 200 people could not get in."[63] Mischief persists, and an 1854 Albany newspaper calls attention to "gunners who violated the laws on Sunday in hunting game and disturbing the neighborhood."[64] Another newspaper reports that "when Albany was flooded in 1857 four wagon loads of provisions and other necessaries were contributed by the Shakers to the sufferers by the high water."[65]

Judge Amasa Parker of Albany befriended the Shakers, and his daughter, Anna (Mrs. John V. L. Pruyn), was a frequent visitor to Watervliet as a young girl. While a student at Albany Female Academy in 1852, she wrote a composition from which we learn of a room full of mulberry boughs where they attempted to cultivate silkworms.[66] The attempt was ultimately unsuccessful because of the climate, although Sister Ann Buckingham's diary suggests that the experiment had earlier met with some success.

American Indians, who must have heard of Shaker charity and may have identified with Shaker family life, wrote for advice on negotiating with the United States government. An 1874 letter from Brethren Samuel Boler, Giles B. Avery, Chauncy Miller, and Benjamin Gates "to our Friends, The Indians of the Sacks, Fox, Kiewar, and Rapahoos" counsels them to send some of their young braves to receive a formal education before attempting to negotiate.[67]

This photograph of Nehemiah White and his boys is probably the work of James Irving of Troy, New York, who made stereopticon views of the Watervliet Shakers from 1861 to 1868. The barefoot boys are dressed like brethren except for waistcoats and braces. Boys were required to work to contribute to the productivity of the farms. Brother Nehemiah, who is shown here standing with hat in hand, was buried at Watervliet in 1887 at the age of 63. (Canterbury Shaker Museum Collection)

Right: *Ten sisters and one brother pose here in the North Family yard (now the site of the Shaker Ridge Country Club) for a stereopticon view probably taken by Irving. From left to right, the buildings (none of which remains) are the wood house, laundry, hired men's house, storage house, barn (at center), wagon shed in far rear, dairy attached to the second house, and the rear of the main dwelling house. Doorway overhangs, or hoods, typical Shaker architectural details, are clearly visible on several of the buildings. (Reproduced courtesy of Gertrude Reno Sherburne)*

Below: *The Church Family sisters' workshop, built in the nineteenth century, was photographed before demolition (ca. 1927) by Edwin J. Stein. (New York State History Collection)*

Right: *North Family quadrangle in winter, ca. 1900. From left to right, the buildings are the wood house, steam and engine house, hired men's house, and barn. (Reproduced courtesy of Gertrude Reno Sherburne)*

The Church Family seed house (left) and mill (below), two other nineteenth-century buildings, were photographed by Stein before demolition ca. 1927. The mill building was the second on the site, the first having been destroyed by fire in 1886. (New York State History Collection)

Right: *Church Family brethren's shop and herb house. A basement datestone establishes that the shop (at left) was built in 1822 by Bruster & Allen. It was remodeled for a nurses residence in 1927. The nineteenth-century herb house beside it was still standing in 1930, when William F. Winter took this photograph. (New York State History Collection)*

Brother Philip Smith was born in 1837 and was buried in Watervliet in 1905. As trustee of the Church Family, he had charge of its business with the world. (Reproduced courtesy of Gertrude Reno Sherburne)

The seed order blank at left, which also advertises brooms, brushes, prepared sweet corn, medicinal herbs, roots, and extracts, asks that orders be addressed to Philip Smith, Shakers, Albany, New York. (New York State Library Collection)

Church Family canning factory and laundry, built 1858. William F. Winter photographed the apparently unused buildings in 1930. The laundry wing is now used by the Ann Lee Home (New York State History Collection)

Right: *Tin can, lid, and label for "Hermetically Sealed" green peas. According to an 1859 account book, the peas were first shelled and "riddled," or put through a coarse sieve. After parboiling, they were placed in tins, and the caps, "perforated [by] a very small hole for ventilation," were soldered onto the cans. The holes were also sealed with solder, but after the cans had been boiled for two hours the holes were touched with the soldering iron to allow the escape of steam. The holes were resoldered, and the cans boiled two hours longer. The specially designed tin cans were manufactured at the Shaker tin shop on the road to the river farm. The label shown here was found among others at the Church Family canning factory, but there is no record of a relationship between the Shakers and Boyle & Dyer. (New York State History Collection)*

Peas, beets, beans, tomatoes, and applesauce were canned by the Shakers for sale to the world. In many instances the name of the trustee was printed on the labels. (New York State History Collection)

Right: *The Church Family sisters in this Irving photograph are (left to right) Lydia Annas, Adelaide Ingham, Eliza Harrison, Katy Ferguson, Julia McNallen, Lucy Fuller, Ruth Green, Maria Treadway, and Samantha Bowie. (New York State History Collection)*

Left: *These young sisters posed for James Irving wearing the Shaker costume commonly worn in the 1860s. The photograph shows two different ways of wearing the kerchief, which was soon after replaced by a shawl collar, or bertha, worn as part of the dress. Seated furthest to the left are the natural sisters Emma and Sarah Neale, who went from Watervliet to Mt. Lebanon. (New York State History Collection)*

John Noyes, an authority on American socialism, stated in 1870 that "the example of the Shakers has demonstrated, not merely that successful Communism is subjectively possible, but that this nation is free enough to let it grow."[68] It is ironic that when the world was "free enough to let it grow" the movement no longer grew. The nineteen communities Shakerism encompassed by 1826 had gradually started to close their doors only fifty years later. As each community was dissolved, its members were absorbed by the remaining communities. The Shaker movement continued to fascinate the world, but those who were fascinated were no longer prospective converts. At Watervliet the pattern of decline in population was definitely set by 1875. Of the total Shaker group of 144 (56 males and 88 females), 23 were under sixteen and 59 were over sixty years of age; a count of 28 hired hands included their families.

Charles Nordhoff noted that "no monument [was] built over the grave of Mother Ann"[69] in 1875, and Charles Dudley Warner, who attempted to find the grave in 1879, was told that "it was the first grave in the sixteenth row from the road on the north side." He found that the graves lay in parallel rows with "little rough slate headstones," but because there was little more than the initials on some to distinguish them, he was never sure if he had found the one he sought.[70]

The earliest illustration of the cemetery, on the 1839 "Plan of Watervliet," indicates room for ten rows (A through J), with all burials prior to 1839 in rows A, B, C, F, I, and J. Mother Ann's grave, F-15, is off-center because most of the burials after 1860 appear in rows K through P to the east of the original yard, probably as a result of a decision to enlarge the cemetery. In November 1872, the Central Shaker Ministry at Mt. Lebanon issued "Burying Ground Directions" to the societies, establishing size and material for markers and the nature of inscriptions. Cemeteries were to be level between stones, kept free from weeds and rubbish, and enclosed with a plain, neat fence.[71] The instructions were duly followed at Watervliet, and a bill for the "Cost of Placing Tombstones, Sept. 1, 1880" (now in the collection of the Western Reserve Historical Society) was apportioned among the four families. Excepting Mother Ann Lee's $6.50 marker, the tombstones cost $456.30 ($1.30 each for 351), and leveling and setting ($1.00 per day) brought the total expenditure to $712.15. (The 1970s replacement cost for a single stone was $236).

Charles Dudley Warner's introduction to the Watervliet village was through the little school, which he visited in summer while girls classes were in session. Although the schoolteacher stated "with fascinating simplicity [that] her school had adopted all the latest educational improvements," Warner concluded that "there was in this school-room a charming atmosphere of content, bounded by a most wholesome ignorance of the world."

Elsewhere he describes an elderly Shaker sister as "erect, vigorous, springy and at 80 performing the labor of a young woman, but there was very little left of her." He observes the sisters at different ages as being in varying stages of mental "starvation, criticism, denial, mortification of the flesh, by which the body — all that is gross in it — was gradually expelled, so that death would be a scarcely perceptible change, and the woman would pass away at last like a dissolving view." As for the children, they lived in an "atmosphere of affectionate care, but of industry." One boy's amusement and work was picking beetles off vines. He saw in the children "already the air of resignation and freedom from excitement" which was apparent in their

Watervliet sisters and Elder George Albert Lomas on a trip, ca. 1880–89. Lomas died in 1889 at the age of 49 — especially early considering the Shaker reputation for longevity. The Shakers in the picture could have been visiting a distant Shaker community, as they often did, or going no further than Albany for a carriage ride. (Canterbury Shaker Museum Collection)

elders. Harsher than most critics, he wrote that he "did not see at Niskeuna any evidence of superior intellectual and moral or spiritual growth in consequence of the pietism which bids us to forget the body" — but it is worth noting in this connection that he did not visit on the Sabbath and consequently did not observe the fervor of worship.[72]

From society to society and from year to year, there had been little change in the appearance or activities of the Shakers. The singing of a canary in an office, an embroidered motto on a wall, and a patchwork cover to break the simplicity of a pine chair (previously forbidden by the Millennial Laws) were perhaps the first indications of the influence of the world.

By the 1880s the Great Gate was opened again to the world, and the roads to Wisdom's Valley were crowded with "curious pleasure-seekers." Regardless of the No Trespassing signs on the grounds, a part of many outings to see the "Shaker Show" was picnicking.

The admonition of the elder in the meeting as to the use of spitboxes was about as strong a reproach as was ever given before it was deemed necessary to close the gate again: "The use of tobacco is a practice not followed by ourselves and we wish to be protected from its effects."[73]

A letter written in 1887 suggests that the world went to the Shaker meetings by invitation only. To Elizabeth Reid, the writer, the Shaker simplicity of design was unattractive — "The Shaker costume was not designed for beauty any more than were their houses. The latter are plain substantially built buildings of brick and wood, without the faintest suggestion of ornamentation." But, she was impressed by the genuine hospitality and "miracles of neatness." She was not willing to exchange her life for one "of continual self-sacrifice and hard work, with little or no play," and stated that "there is little in their lives that is attractive to persons of worldly minds." To her the Shakers were "honest, sober, industrious and sincere" and might afford a "welcome haven to persons weary of the world."[74]

Aside from the world's visitors the Shakers continued to travel among themselves. A "Programme of Eastern Journey," written by Giles B. Avery in 1866, makes one incredulous of his stamina and doubtful of his explanation that "we cannot vary over one day from above, unless compelled so to do, by accident or sickness, or unknown burdens."[75]

The West Family journals from 1885 to 1898 tell the story of continuing labor and decreasing numbers, with the exception of arrivals who temporarily swelled the ranks at Wisdom's Valley when the Groveland Shaker community near Rochester closed in 1892. Among entries for 1886, we find "Eldress A & the older part (10 in number) take a sleigh ride," later, that the "Church saw and grist mill burned (about $10,000) so one calamity follows another," and of Brother John L. Decker's funeral, "this is the last of the aged burden bearers." The record for 1888 starts with the count of "all told 5 brethren and 14 sisters."[76]

The census of 1892 — taken on 16 February 1892 before the arrival of the Groveland Shakers — accounts for 116 individuals at Watervliet, 23 of whom are probably hired men and families, which leaves 93 Shakers (28 males and 65 females).

This Watervliet spirit drawing of ca. 1882 was "Written and Presented [to] the Second Family of Shakers By Eugene Cunningham." Although the age of spiritual manifestations ended by the mid-eighteenth century, some isolated later spirit drawings are known. It is possible that Eugene Cunningham was the instrument through which this message was received as well as the brother who executed it. His name does not appear among Watervliet census data, nor is he buried at Watervliet. (Elmer R. Pearson Collection)

Left margin notes:

```
Math - 32 × 64 clmp - 64 × 64 149
Gift - 3/4 × 6 + = 52
80.8 rods
16.67" = 35
```

	A	B	C	D	E	F	G	H	I	J	K	L	M	N
1	Benj'n Youngs D.1818 A.82	John McNeerin D.1820 A.53	Polly Bates D.1823 A.35	Ozias Turney D.1841 A.39	Betsy Lovegrove D.1808 A.47	Patty Robbins D.1791 A.27	Clarissa Vedder D.1857 A.65	Lucy Brown D.1844 A.45	Rhoda Chase D.1833 A.78	Timothy Hubbard D.1814 A.72	Elizabeth Train D.1865 A.72	Hosea Fuller D.1866 A.91	Jos C. Buckingham D.1880 A.82	George A Lome D.1889 A.49
2	Mary E Mills D.1824	Anna Carter D.1820 A.66	Mary Mills D.1828 A.64	Dan'l Arrants D.1841 A.21	Ann Potter D.1854 A.84	Noamo Southwick D.1806 A.43	Merrell Baker D.1859 A.83	Anna Benedict D.1845 A.76	Mary Partington D.1833 A.78	Ja's Ostrander D.1814 A.71	Ja's Ostrander D.1866 A.72	David Cole D.1866 A.64	Fredric Frank D.1881 A.82	Aurilla White D.1889 A.71
3	Boney Burch D.1831 A.65	Margaret White D.1822 A.67	John Ball D.1856 A.10	Hanh A Latimers D.1822 A.22	Joseph Hodgson D.1854 A.93	Wm Bigsby D.1781 A.53	Fred S Wicker D.1859 A.63	Jonath Slosson D.1845 A.85	David Osborn D.1834 A.80	Anna Cook D.1872	Ja's Chapman D.1872	Elizabeth Seely	Phebe Lane D.1889 A.84	George Hoffgens D.1889 A.84
4	Arm Remer D.1834 A.40	Anna Bates D.1825 A.15	Lorina Bates D.1828 A.68	Mary Wells D.1842 A.86	Eliz'h Ostrander D.1854 A.93	Priscilla Fitch D.1813 A.78	Sally Taylor D.1859 A.85	Arch'b'd Meacham D.1845 A.66	Anna Simson D.1834 A.65	Elizabeth Goodrich D.1818 A.42	Lucy Horton D.1873	Asa Seaton D.1867 A.74	Laura Prentiss D.1889 A.67	Chauncey Dibbi D.1889 A.67
5	Nehemiah White D.1834 A.53	Elizabeth Younghans D.1825 A.24	Cecelia O'Connor D.1829 A.43	Susan'h Carr D.1842 A.12	John O Neal D.1855 A.53	Benj'n Osborn D.1798 A.39	Francis Goodrich D.1859 A.84	Lucy Prescott D.1845 A.79	Aaron Wood D.1836 A.80	Abig'l S. Butler D.1821 A.26	Emeline Clark D.1873 A.78	Joseph Pelham D.1867 A.74	Ann M Reynolds D.1882 A.78	Lucy A Fairch D.1890 A.82
6	Molly Chapman D.1840 A.93	Electa Case D.1825 A.80	Jason Harwood D.1829 A.71	Hannah Train D.1852 A.86	Wilson Youngs D.1846 A.89	Benj'n S Youngs D.1855 A.80	Channing Prentis D.1859 A.54	Nancy Wells D.1846 A.75	Patience Chase D.1836 A.82	Hezk'h Rowland D.1823 A.67	Patience Earl D.1867 A.78	Louisa Fairchild D.1882 A.78	Chauncey Copely	George B Pric D.1890 A.71
7	Bethuel Shout D.1854 A.17	Abagail Wells D.1826 A.85	Abig'l Wells Jr D.1830 A.49	Ann H. Goff D.1842 A.19	M. Kiersey D.1855 A.7		Abia Crary D.1860 A.75	Wm. Yearsley D.1846 A.69	Peter Dodge D.1833 A.83	Abijah Wood D.1825 A.48	Daniel Brainard D.1874 A.81	Justice Harwood D.1867 A.78	Aaron Sunburg D.1883 A.23	Jessie M Sma D.1891 A.15
8	Phebe Richmond D.1858 A.84	Wm. Carter D.1828 A.84	Jane Thomas D.1830 A.23	Sam'l Heavers D.1843 A.21	Fanny Waterman D.1855 A.77		Cynthia Sherman D.1860 A.71	Polly Vedder D.1846 A.52	Bathsheba Shays D.1838 A.57	Dan'l Wood D.1824 A.88	Jesse Harwood D.1874 A.74	Asenath Pennington D.1868 A.19	Andrew Wood D.1883 A.69	James Langria D.1891 A.72
9	Jos Youngs D.1862 A.25	Olive Butler D.1826 A.30	Olive Wicks D.1852 A.73	Tho's Wells Jr D.1843 A.74	My A Whittaker D.1855 A.55		Abig'l Lemin D.1860 A.81	Theodore Bates D.1860 A.81 (PINE TREE) Seth D Fairchild D.1825 A.17	Lucy Blanchard D.1855 A.72	Wm. Hunter D.1875	Joseph Le Fuma D.1868	Eleanor Vedder D.1883 A.94		Catherine Vedde
10	Chas H Winson D.1861	Deb'h Younghans D.1826 A.20	Rebecca Bates D.1831 A.36	Molly Youngs D.1844 A.90	Elizabeth Bowser D.1855 A.90		Eunice Johnson D.1861 A.80	Dean O. Gage D.1846 A.82	Loanna Gresh D.1838 A.83	Lucy Waterman D.1825 A.86	Lucy Fuller D.1875 A.61	Hester Gustin D.1869 A.56	Elizabeth Barker D.1884 A.52	Caty Ferguson D.1891 A.55
11		Peggy Thomas D.1827 A.29	Elizah Hodgson D.1832 A.76	Betsey Robbins D.1845 A.62	Sam'l Clark D.1855 A.27		Eliza Ash D.1861 A.50	John Scott D.1846 A.80	Clarissa Buckingham D.1841 A.68	Mary Hocknell D.1825 A.66	Mary Hathaway D.1875 A.73	D. M. Treadway D.1869 A.58	Augustus Blask D.1884 A.70	Nathaniel Frye D.1892 A.88
12		Hanh Hosford D.1804 A.65	Levi Derrin D.1832 A.46	E. A Bradley D.1845 A.5	Ann Lowe D.1857 A.47	EL Abiather Babbit D.1847 A.85	Ezekial Copely D.1861 A.91	Nancy White D.1847 A.32	Joanna Bennett D.1838 A.77	Nathan Spier D.1827 A.52	Albert Triss D.1875 A.78	Zeviah Spoir D.1869 A.88	Ann Clement D.1884 A.84	Samantha Bamh D.1892 A.5
13		Susannah Barney D.1797 A.56	Lois Wicks D.1832 A.16	Asa Sigsby D.1845 A.49	Marg't Reid D.1857 A.17	EL John Hocknell D.1799 A.76	Anna Cole D.1847 A.40	Angeline Annas D.1847 A.58	Anna Bennett D.1847 A.80	Eunice Bennett D.1827 A.91	Issachar Bates D.1875 A.72	Desire Butler D.1884 A.72	Paulina Bates D.1892 A.8	Thomas Beal D.1892 A.8
14		Abt Amblaide D.1833	Anna Wells D.1832 A.38	Marg't Latimore D.1846 A.20	Abig'l White D.1857 A.71	EL William Lee D.1784 A.44	Electa Talmadge D.1861 A.57	Benj'n Train D.1847 A.58	Hart'l Clary D.1836 A.14	Almira Wicker D.1827 A.34	Almira Watkins D.1875 A.70	EDWARD POWERS D.1872 A.71	Elizabeth & Harrison D.1885 A.73	Bessie Clark D.1892 A.17
15		David Cole D.1797 A.27	Mary Prentis D.1832 A.68	Ada Manchester D.1846 A.10	Sally Biglow 15 D.1858 A.52	MOTHER ANN LEE Born near Manchester ENGLAND FEB.29,1736 Died in Watervliet N.Y. SEPT. 8, 1784	Robt Bernard D.1862 A.45	Prudence Spencer D.1850 A.75	Angeline Prentis D.1839 A.31	Ruth Clary D.1828 A.91	Jesse Wells D.1876 A.97	Betsy Wells D.1870 A.94	Electa Thomas D.1885 A.84	Phebe R Buckingham D.1892 A.86
16		Amos Hammond Jr D.1797 A.17	Almira Thomas D.1832 A.21	Elizah Malley D.1846 A.11	O J Landers D.1858 A.11	M. Lucy Wright D.1862 A.86	Hannah Wells D.1851 A.13	Betty E Sherman D.1845 A.85	Mary Robinson D.1839 A.66	Susank Cook D.1828 A.57	Abigail Messenger D.1870 A.62	Benj'n Hughbs D.1870 A.83	Almira Treadway D.1893 A.92	George Bussell D.1893 A.92
17		Rachel Lyon D.1835 A.77	Ann Bryant D.1832 A.20	Salathi Thomas D.1847 A.82	H. M. Landers D.1858 A.9	Eli Ruth Landon D.1850 A.74	Wm. Seely D.1863 A.72	Mar. J. Bates D.1851 A.13	Dorathy Kibbee D.1839 A.66	Elizabeth Farrington D.1828 A.56	B. Ann Hankins D.1876 A.84	Charlotte Youngs D.1870 A.83	D. A. Buckingham D.1885 A.82	Stanton Buckingham D.1894 A.92
18		Betty Lane D.1836 A.19	Betsy Bryant D.1833 A.19	Caleb Bates D.1848 A.73	Jos Tearney D.1858 A.66	Eld. Giles & Avery D.1890 A.75	Luther Wells D.1863 A.89	Joseph Preston D.1851 A.84	Gideon Cole D.1840 A.84	Harriet Copley D.1828 A.18	Gordon Horton D.1876 A.86	Polly Ostrander D.1870	Pamelia J Kiersey D.1885 A.69	Burdett Hanks D.1894 A.92
19		Hanh Thompson D.1793 A.99	Beulah Downs D.1837 A.69	Betsey Clark D.1848 A.71	Ann C Damp D.1858 A.57	ELS CAROLINE TATE D.1937 A.78	Lucy Pierce D.1863 A.48	Chloe Wood D.1851 A.74	Loisa M. Smith D.1840 A.10	Seth C Buckingham D.1877 A.24	Zephrm Prentis D.1875 A.8	Joel Smith D.1870	Sarah Taylor D.1885 A.69	Mary French D.1894 A.80
20		Hanh Hocknell D.1795 A.74	F. W. Coary D.1837	Mercy Everitt D.1849 A.71	David Train Jr D.1858 A.81	ELLA MYER 20 D.1937 A.61	Desire Harwood D.1863 A.65	Asenath Harwood D.1851 A.57	L. M. Campbell D.1840 A.10	Anna M Dole D.1828 A.20	Ruth Green D.1877 A.61 (Holt)	Alce Remer D.1871 A.69	John L. Decker D.1886 A.72	Susan Love D.1894 A.80
21		David Preston D.1789 A.26	Geo Leonard D.1838	A.E German D.1849 A.20	Eunice Copley D.1858 A.76	ELS ANNA CASB 21	Simon Smith D.1863 A.64	David Miller D.1852 A.77	Betsey Hastings D.1840 A.8	Fanny Sherman D.1829 A.23	John Holt D.1877 A.68	Harriet Hutchison D.1871 A.63	Fidial Hotheway D.1886 A.83	Jennet Angus D.1894 A.84
22		Jos Bennett Sen D.1788 A.67	Betsey Carter D.1830 A.21	Angus McFee D.1853 A.81	Susank Youngs D.1853 A.33	ELS ANNA CASB D.1938 A.83	Oscar Merchant D.1863 A.21	Calvin Wells D.1852 A.77	Catharine Hemer D.1834 A.53	Susan Hemington D.1877 A.63	Polly Turner D.1877 A.63	Fregift Wells D.1877 A.63	Nehemiah White D.1895 A.70	Jacob Baur D.1895 A.70
23		Violet Bennett D.1785 A.25	Lydia Gear D.1838 A.27	Walter Waterman D.1851 A.81	Jos Turner D.1800 A.60		Charlotte Gale D.1863 A.43	Abig'l Shapley D.1853 A.78	N.C. Clary D.1841 A.13	Henry Younghont D.1831 A.20	Permilla Earl D.1878 A.75	Mercy Harwood D.1871 A.78	Wm. C Brackett D.1887 A.80	Caroline Downs D.1895 A.92
24		Benj'n Youngs Jr D.1820 A.40	Tho's Turney D.1838 A.83	M.A. Riley D.1851	Elisha Bartow D.1800 A.47		Polly Wicks D.1863 A.77	Ruth Johnson D.1854 A.89	Susan A. Green D.1842 A.20	Sam'l Chase D.1821 A.65	Sam'l Gould D.1878 A.49	Richard Dean D.1871 A.73	Lovina Soulisbury D.1887 A.65	Nancy Wicks D.1895 A.92
25	HARRY RICHMOND D.1925 A.87	Mary Whittaker D.1815 A.83	Jonathan Mills D.1821 A.79	Tho's Conroy D.1851	Marg't Harwood D.1859 A.63		Stephen Wells D.1864 A.88	Arthosa White D.1854 A.69	Hannah Prescott D.1831 A.18	Cynthia Wicks D.1878 A.80	Irena Bates D.1878	Caroline Ulrich D.1881 A.83	Galen Richmond D.1887 A.83	Almira Teachout D.1895 A.72
26	JAMES STALKER D.1907 A.75	Calvin H Wells D.1833 A.17	Anna Carter Jr D.1833 A.58	Benj'n Wells D.1851 A.81	Tina Seaton D.1860 A.78		Jos Mathins D.1864 A.81	Susanh Green D.1854 A.71	Sarah Bennett D.1843 A.73	Mercy Boothe D.1832 A.70	Jos J Lone D.1878 A.80	Marg't Lanure D.1871	Abram Ellis D.1887 A.74	Henry Murry D.1895 A.72
27	Margaret Poddock D.1873 A.45	Wm. Clark D.1809 A.42	Wm Davidson D.1839 A.68	Jonathan Cole D.1851 A.84	Ann Bowser D.1860 A.74		Abrm Hendrickson D.1864 A.94	Judith Bishop D.1855 A.85	Jacob C. Green D.1843 A.64	Jos Buckingham D.1832 A.70	Mariah Gillett D.1879 A.80	Jos Goodnew D.1882 A.84	John Randolph D.1888 A.75	Alexander Miln D.1897 A.86
28	Jno C Carter D.1801 A.27	Alvira Brown D.1836 A.15	Ralph Hodgson D.1840 A.96	Jane Beall D.1852 A.86	Hannah Youngs D.1860 A.83		Sarah A Wood D.1865 A.29	Judith Rich D.1855 A.85	Mary Mulley D.1834 A.53	Elizabth Shays D.1838 A.53	Shubal Prentis D.1879 A.75	David Hankins D.1872 A.55	Sylvester Prentiss D.1890 A.75	William Bussel D.1897 A.80
29	Lucy Pease D.1820 A.39	Philena Carter D.1803 A.33	Dolly Harwood D.1849 A.89	Jos Chapman D.1849 A.89	Sarah Beall D.1849 A.89		Phebe Taylor D.1849 A.89	Jane Hodgson D.1843 A.78	Nathan Slosson D.1843 A.78	Levi Pease D.1880 A.77	Martha Bates D.1880 A.77	Phebe A Smith D.1872 A.55	Charles Pretch D.1888 A.72	Lydia Dol D.1897 A.55
30	Luther Morse D.1815 A.12	Rebecca Carter D.1866 A.79	Mary Allen D.1841 A.26	Martin Rastett D.1852 A.52	Polly Bacon D.1861 A.72	Hezek'h Noble D.1792 A.32	Elizabeth Youngs D.1865 A.82	Azuba Train D.1857 A.64	Alex. Brown D.1833 A.87	Eliza Wells D.1862 A.84	Alex. Youngs D.1872 A.56	Rachel Webb D.1888 A.64	Lydia Annas D.1897 A.52	

Bottom axis: A 42   B   C   D   E   F   I   G   H   I   J   K   L   M   N

Bottom notes: 25.85 × 209' — 5 rods

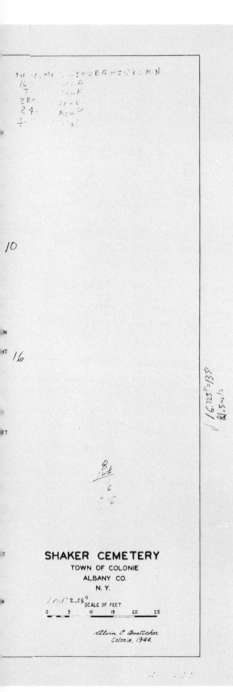

SHAKER CEMETERY

TOWN OF COLONIE
ALBANY CO.
N. Y.

SCALE OF FEET

0   5   10   15   20   25

Alvin P. Boettcher
Colonie, 1944.

Left: *Chart of the Watervliet Shaker cemetery made by Alvin P. Boettcher in 1944. Boettcher, who knew the Watervliet Shakers well, spent most of his later life studying the history of the Shakers. The significance of the different lettering on the right is not known. The rough annotations are Boettcher's. (Town of Colonie Historical Society Collection)*

Originally buried on land which did not belong to the Shakers, Mother Ann's body was later disinterred and replaced in the Shaker burying ground. It was not until 1880 that the gravestones were placed there,

uniform in size and simply marked with the name, date of death, and the age of the deceased, excepting the larger stone of the founder, which reads: "Mother/ Ann Lee/ Born in Manchester/ England/ Feb. 29, 1736/ Died in Watervliet, N.Y./ Sept. 8, 1784." The photograph above was taken ca. 1925. In recent years the original stone was replaced with a new one of the same design. (Emma B. King Library, Shaker Museum, Old Chatham)

Sister Adelaide Ingham, who died at Watervliet in 1927 at the age of 94, is shown here seated in a Shaker chair in front of the hitching posts at the Church Family Great Gate ca. 1890, when the pipe and granite posts had replaced the original wooden hitch-ups. (Reproduced courtesy of Francis Spoonogle)

Right: This unidentified Watervliet sister posed for her portrait in the photographer's studio during the 1880s — reflecting relaxation of regulations on the ownership or display of pictures, especially framed ones. (New York State History Collection)

This 1886 photograph records sisters identified as Ellie, Barbara [Hooper] holding Sambo, and Samantha [Bowie]. All three sisters are wearing the shawl collars which supplanted the earlier kerchiefs, and Samantha adds a world-style jabot and reticule. Household pets are another new development forbidden by earlier Millennial Laws. (New York State History Collection)

NEW YORK.—THE SHAKERS AT LEBANON—THE SINGING MEETING.—FROM A SKETCH BY JOSEPH BECKER.—SEE PAGE 286.

THE SHAKERS IN NISKAYUNA.

THE SHAKERS IN NISKAYUNA.—THE SINGING MEETING.

*This engraving of "The Shakers in
Niskayuna — The Singing Meeting," which
appeared in* Frank Leslie's Popular Monthly
*in 1885, was actually a recutting of the Mt.
Lebanon illustration shown above. In the
later publication no credit is given to the
artist. By 1885 kerchiefs and bonnet strings
had been eliminated from the sisters'
costume.*

MINK'S POPULAR SHAKERS HOTEL.

In the 1880s an alternative to picnicking on the lawn, for those who could afford it, was a pleasant drive to the Shaker meeting, buying a few water lilies from a backslider, and then returning for dinner at George E. Mink's Popular Shakers Hotel. (Thomas Vareday Collection)

In this ca. 1900 photograph, the Shakers Hotel is identified as Powell's Inn. Later it became Duncan's Inn, and it is now known as Vittles & Grog. (Town of Colonie Historical Society Collection)

The picture of Eldress Anna White dressed for travel contrasts sharply with the fashion of the world. (Reproduced courtesy of Marian Curtis Kunz)

The woodcut beside her, from F. W. Beers's 1876 Atlas of Rensselaer County, depicts a home in Greenbush Heights, opposite Albany, which reflects the contemporary standard of taste. In the words of Elizabeth Reid, "the Shaker costume was not designed for beauty any more than their houses."

Left: Elder Giles B. Avery, a regular visiting elder from the Central Ministry at Mt. Lebanon, was buried in Watervliet after succumbing to an illness there in 1890 at the age of 75. This photograph was taken by Irving when Avery was in his late forties. The consideration Shakers showed each other in the face of great hardship is expressed in a journal at the time of his death. An entry for 27 December reads, "Elder Giles died at 1:40 p.m. I helped lay him out & then start for New Lebanon to let them know." On 28 December the writer records, "I started from Hancock for Lebanon. Took 4 yoke oxen to break road. I followed with a horse. Snows & blows. After notifying the Church Elders I return to Hancock and get as far as Alb." And on 30 December he writes, "Attend Elder Giles funeral at 9 am. 12 from Lebanon & 8 from Hancock & Enfield were present. A solemn time." (New York State History Collection)

George Albert Lomas (1840–89) was an elder of the South Family at an early age. He edited Plain Talks, *a pamphlet, and* The Shaker, *a newspaper published by the Shakers at Watervliet in 1871 and 1872. After a fire in 1873 the paper was issued from Mt. Lebanon, edited by Frederick Evans, and renamed* Shaker and Shakeress. *In 1876 and 1877 it was again published at Watervliet with Lomas as editor. Throughout this period it had wide circulation among public libraries as well as within Shaker communities. (Emma B. King Library, Shaker Museum, Old Chatham)*

Lomas is shown at top left seated at his desk in the Watervliet printing office surrounded by copies of The Shaker *on the racks. (Fruitlands Museum, Harvard, Mass.) In the lower photograph of elders of the*

South Family in 1870, No. 1 is identified as Elder George Albert Lomas, and No. 4 as Eldress Harriet Bullard. The other two are unidentified. (Western Reserve Historical Society Collection)

Sister Ella Winship (ca. 1890–1900) was one of the Groveland Shakers who came to live at the North Family. She became a teacher at the District School No. 14 as early as 1895 and continued to teach for many years, moving to the South Family in 1915, when the North Family closed. Later, she moved to Mt. Lebanon, where she became an eldress. Although the kerchief she wears here was not common in this period, we occasionally find sisters wearing it for special occasions or when posing for portraits. (Reproduced courtesy of Gertrude Reno Sherburne)

Right: Elder Isaac Anstatt of the West Family, ca. 1900, and Brother Isaac Anstatt photographed as a young man by James Irving (New York State History Collection)
As elder, Isaac Anstatt had a variety of responsibilities at the West Family. He is still remembered today as the Shaker elder who delivered butter and eggs to Albany. (The more recent photo is reproduced courtesy of Marian Curtis Kunz)

Eldress Polly Lee came to Watervliet in 1892, when the Groveland community near Rochester, New York, was dissolved and the Groveland Shakers found a new home at the Watervliet North Family. Because of a facial neuralgia Eldress Polly always wore a face scarf. (Western Reserve Historical Society Collection)

In the 1894 photograph at left Eldress Anna Case is shown cutting the ends off corncobs with a machine almost identical to the Amsterdam broom cutter below it. The girls then stripped the corn. At least two girls in the picture later became Shaker sisters — Mary Dahm (seated next to Eldress Anna) and Grace Dahm (third from left). (New York State History Collection)

Although the Shakers attempted to make everything for themselves, they did buy from the world. This broom cutter, which produced an even edge on the finished broom, was made in Amsterdam, New York, about twenty-five miles from the Watervliet community. (Collection Shakertown at Pleasant Hill, Kentucky)

Below: *North Family bean pickers, ca. 1900. Journal entries for 1894 establish the volume of string beans picked and processed — 126 dozen cans "put up" on 10 August, 80 dozen on 15 August, 93 dozen on 19 August, 65 dozen on 21 August — in all, 4,368 cans. In this snapshot Eldress Polly Lee is standing in the center foreground. Sister Jennie Lee is on the left behind her, and Esther Relyea is kneeling next to Sister Jennie. (Reproduced courtesy of Marian Curtis Kunz)*

Left: *Walnut bureau, attributed to Brother Emmory Brooks, of the Groveland community, ca. 1850. In 1943 Sister Jennie Wells wrote to Dr. Charles C. Adams of the New York State Museum that Emmory Brooks "made all the [Groveland] Sisters a black walnut bedstead," and enclosed a 6 January 1869 letter to Eldress Polly Lee at Groveland in which Brother Emmory had written from Enfield: "I am coming home after a while to finish your bedstead so do not let others medle with it or try to have it finished before I return." (New York State History Collection)*

Although the 1930 Winter photograph above is supposed to depict Eldress Anna Case's bedroom at the South Family, adopted children of the family at the turn of the century do not remember the room shown as hers. In any case, it does contain a bed which once belonged to Eldress Polly Lee of the North Family. The bed and bureau of black walnut were made by Emmory Brooks. Oilcloth, linoleum, fringe on the Shaker chairs, and calendar pictures reflect the encroachment of the world on the Shaker aesthetic. (New York State History Collection)

SOUTH FAMILY.

1900–1925

By 1905 the total population of Wisdom's Valley was seventy-seven, ten of whom were probably hired men and families. Of the total, there were seventeen males including the hired hands; of this number seven were over sixty, and seven were under sixteen. In records kept at Mt. Lebanon by order of the Central Ministry, the 1916 annual report shows wages paid to hired men and women as over $4,500. The effects of the industrial revolution were felt increasingly as the Shakers were unable to compete with a mechanized world.

The Shakers moved from one society to another at the direction of the Central Ministry. The change could be a disciplinary measure, or a leavening of ages or sexes. Most often the reasons are unknown.

By this time the real estate pendulum had swung, and the recorded transactions are for sales rather than purchases of Shaker property. Before the sales began, the family holdings around the Shaker village amounted to approximately 2,000 acres: Church, 773.5; North, 383.5; South, 444.3; West, 400.7. Many small parcels were sold to individuals; names of neighbors are among those one can recognize — Lothridge, Orlop, Freligh, Male — and also names of persons who once worked for the Shakers, such as former foremen Schairer and Strobel.

Most of our information about the last thirty-eight years of the Shakers at Wisdom's Valley comes from persons living today who worked for the Shakers as young men, or whose fathers and grandfathers had. Many of the homes and farms around the perimeter of the Albany County Airport are still owned by families who knew the Shakers as friends.

Besides making fancy goods which were sold at the South Family shop, the sisters contracted to finish shirts for a Troy manufacturer. One of the world's children later remarked, "We crocheted everything for fancy goods — you name it, we did it." From left to right are Sisters Mary Dahm, Maggie Caldwell, and May King, Eldress Anna Case, and Sister Frieda Sipple. (New York State History Collection)

Walter Engel, whose great grandmother Teresa Engel once cooked for forty-five men working on Shaker Island, still lives on the farm his ancestors moved to in 1871. As a young man, Engel himself worked for the Shakers cutting wood or ice. For many years he was a friend of the last elder at the Church Family, Josiah Barker, and spent a great deal of time reminiscing with him.

It was Elder Josiah who told him about sod fences and "woodchuck Shakers." The mounds of earth crisscrossing the area around the village like entrenchments were actually sod fences used to designate property lines. When property was added, the old fences were not destroyed but simply added to. Much of this work was done by what Josiah called woodchuck Shakers — his term for "winter Shakers," who were ostensibly joining the Shakers but were actually securing a winter's lodging, only to leave in the spring.

Years later, Engel, with the knowledge he had received from Elder Josiah, was able to assist surveyors working on airport boundaries who, as he described the scene, were standing with a bushel basket full of deeds trying to find a "point of beginning."

Elder Josiah also said, obviously with a twinkle in his eye, that Shakers were lazy people. They never did anything themselves that they could invent a machine to do for them. About 1917 he sold the huge ⅜-inch-thick copper still in which the Shakers had made their cider (the Millennial Laws' only restriction on cider was that it should be under lock and key). The still had been dismantled at the time of the Civil War when the government imposed a tax of $1,000 per still.

Several members of the Willey family are still commercial farmers in the area. Descendants of Bert Willey, once foreman at the North Family, three of them were born at Watervliet. They were delivered by Dr. Lothridge, who was also the doctor for the Shakers for many years. Their mother told them that he had charged $2.50 for each delivery. One of these children, Frank, remembers today the industries still in operation at Watervliet in the early 1900s: canning beets, tomatoes, and beans; broommaking at the North Family; and growing broomcorn on the island. When corn was growing they walked along and bent the heads over their arms to make it easier to harvest. All that was harvested for brooms was the brush, or tassel, of the stalks. In 1914 the state of New York appropriated Shaker land along the Mohawk River for a barge canal, thereby almost flooding the Shaker islands. Willey sawed wood for the steam machine which did the wash at the South Family. "They used a gourd dipper to get soft soap out of the big cauldron."

Another neighbor, Miss Edith Wasmuth, has lived in the same house opposite the Church Family property since 1895. As a child she skated on the Ann Lee Pond and then warmed herself by the kitchen stove and talked to the sisters. She recalls the team of oxen passing her house on their way to the river farm.

Fred Tribley was hired by the Shakers to help with vegetable canning. He operated a machine for rolling on the can tops, rented from the American Canning Company. His father learned to make tin cans at the Shaker shop when he came from England to the Church Family at the age of sixteen. When Albany County purchased the Church Family property in 1926, the sawmill was slated to be torn down. Fred took down the mill and used the lumber to build his home on what is now Route 7.

This was a period when the Shakers' main responsibility was caring for the world's children, most of whom would later return to the world. As a result, the greatest source of information about Wisdom's Valley comes from women who lived there as children during the early 1900s: Trude Reno, Martha Mailander, Marguerite Putnam, the Relyea sisters, the Cross sisters went to the Shakers as the result of misfortune in their own families. They were treated with stern but affectionate care, and all, after returning to the world, remarked about an overwhelming homesickness. Their random recollections recapture some part of what they experienced — "We were not allowed to go near the hired men"; "Sister Jennie Wells used to pinch for punishment"; "we were not allowed toys outside of our rooms"; "some were retarded children . . . made to feel one of the Family"; "sometimes we could stay up in summer to see the fireflies"; "we tied an American flag on Tippy's tail [Sister Jennie Wells's dog] for the Fourth of July"; "we trick-or-treated at Halloween — had a huge bonfire and dressed up in old clothes"; "we had to shake the snow off our blankets in the morning. We did not mind the cold and slept with the windows wide open in the depth of winter"; and "we took turns (four weeks at a time) kitchen, dining room, dairy, hen house, men's dining room. We worked a lot, but it never hurt us."

Watervliet Shaker School District No. 14, located on the Church Family property, is remembered by children from the North and West Families as late as 1912. The Cross sisters, who first went to the Shakers in 1914, remember going to school on the South Family property in a building which was also used as the carpenter's shop. The South Family school, also referred to as School District No. 14, closed in 1926. According to Mrs. Edwin Thomas, who was the last teacher at that school, there were two girls from the South Family in her class, and the remaining six students, both boys and girls, were children of tenant farmers.

In 1927 the original School District No. 14, built in 1823, was to be demolished and the Ann Lee Home power station erected on the site. There is a difference of opinion as to whether the original foundation was reused and, indeed, whether the building was simply remodeled.

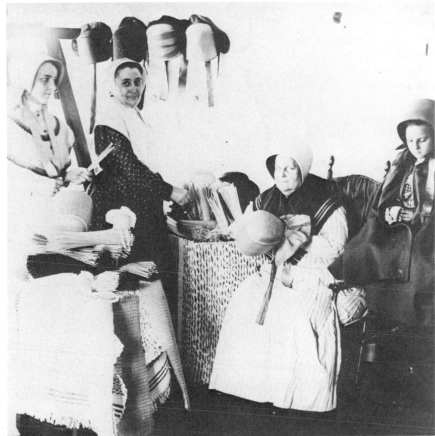

Bert Willey, North Family foreman, was one of the men on whom the Shakers depended for the smooth operation of their farms. He is shown here with his wife and three of their children (Frank, Lou, and Edward) who were born at the North Family. All of these children were delivered by the world's Dr. Lothridge, a man devoted to the Shakers and they to him. Mrs. Willey, years later, told Frank that Dr. Lothridge's charge for delivering was $2.50. (Reproduced courtesy of Lou Willey Hillard)

The carefully posed photograph of South Family members making bonnets was probably taken in the early years of the twentieth century when Shakers posed for postal cards. From left to right are Sister Grace Dahm, Ethel Milton (a non-Shaker), Sister Eva Larkin, Laura Milton (a non-Shaker), and Loretta Milton (a non-Shaker), who is holding a Shaker doll bonnet. (Reproduced courtesy of Marian Curtis Kunz)

The South Family reading group, ca. 1908, is obviously posed for a postal card. The Shaker stove is in sharp contrast to the world's wicker chair. (Reproduced courtesy of Gertrude Reno Sherburne)

Group pictures of this period, some of which were posed for postal cards, rarely showed members of only one family — remaining brethren being so greatly outnumbered by the sisters that for appearance' sake they posed in all family pictures. Elder Josiah Barker of the Church Family appears at right in the middle row of the 1910 South Family picture seated next to Elder Isaac Anstatt of the West Family. George Duncan, who appears and reappears in conventional world clothing, worked for the Shakers but was not a member.

Above: *North Family at their dwelling house with visitors from South and Church Families, ca. 1905. This picture was probably taken on the Sabbath, as most of the group are dressed in white. Ordinarily, the Shakers did not take in babies or very young children, and Trude Reno, the child shown seated in the center, was an exception. Trude went to the Shakers in 1903 and was entrusted to the care of her natural mother during her few years there. A visitor from the world can be distinguished by her elegant hat. (Reproduced courtesy of Gertude Reno Sherburne)*

Below: *North Family group, ca. 1912. Seated left to right are Elder Josiah Barker of the Church Family, Eldresses Lavinia Dutcher and Polly Lee, and Sister Jennie Wells. Standing left to right are Esther Relyea, Irene Coburn, and Sisters Agnes Stebbins and Ella Winship. Sister Jennie's dog, Tippy, is beside Elder Josiah Barker. (Reproduced courtesy of Gertrude Reno Sherburne)*

Above: *South Family group, ca. 1908.*
(Reproduced courtesy of Francis
Spoonogle). Right: *South Family group, ca.*
1910. (Reproduced courtesy of Gertrude
Reno Sherburne)

Sister Jennie Wells came to the North Family at Watervliet from Groveland in 1892. She moved to the South Family when the North Family was closed in 1915, and remained there to within a few years of the closing of the Watervliet community, when she moved to Hancock. (Reproduced courtesy of Marian Curtis Kunz)

North Family children, ca. 1905. Left to right are Katherine Relyea, Julia Relyea, and Esther Relyea. Sister Jennie Wells was the caretaker of these children. (Reproduced courtesy of Marian Curtis Kunz)

The world's children who recalled their Shaker schooling observed that "the North Family children envied the South Family because of a more relaxed life," and that "Eldress Anna Case, was not as strict as Eldress Polly [Lee]." This photograph of Eldress Anna was taken ca. 1910. (New York State History Collection)

In the above photograph of the Church Family school taken ca. 1905, Sister Ella Winship stands at the rear beside the door. Girls classes were originally held in the summer and boys classes in the winter, but by the twentieth century the distinction no longer existed. (Reproduced courtesy of Marian Curtis Kunz)

In 1913 Rachel and Grant McDonald, whose widowed father forsook millions at the death of his young wife, were sent to their Aunt Rachel, then eldress at the West Family in Watervliet. The dramatic story was publicized in the Albany Knickerbocker Press. Grant, later to be an engineer at the General Electric Company in Schenectady, appears in this snapshot of the 1913 District No. 14 class at upper left, next to Sister Ella. Rachel is in the upper center with her head bowed. (Reproduced courtesy of Gertrude Reno Sherburne)

On sleds hitched together, some of the world's children enjoy sleigh-riding at the South Family during a recess from school and fancywork. Left to right are Victoria Cross, Mabel Cassel, Martha Mailander, Gertrude Cross, Catherine Cross, and Marguerite Putnam, who were cared for by the Shakers in the early 1900s. (Reproduced courtesy of Gertrude Reno Sherburne)

North Family Shakers with visitors, ca. 1905. Perhaps this group was heading for a picnic. Frank Leslie's Illustrated Newspaper *had reported of this popular activity in 1873, "Then again they have picnics in the Summer months — queer Shaker picnics, with plenty to eat, and plenty of water and lemonade to drink, but without a bit of flirtation — heaven save the mark!" (Reproduced courtesy of Gertrude Reno Sherburne)*

South Family sewing room. The maple stair rail built in the South Family dwelling house in 1800 can be seen through the sewing room doorway in William F. Winter's 1930 photograph. Along with some other traditional Shaker furnishings, it is in sharp contrast to the scrollwork in the arch as well as the clock and linoleum that reflect the contemporary world's taste. In the alcove a yardstick and multiple coat hanger are hung on the pegboard next to the early Shaker stove. The walnut counter probably came from Groveland. (New York State History Collection)

1925–1938

In 1925 it was no longer necessary to turn to a census enumerator for a count of the Shakers. They could be counted on the fingers of two hands. The West Family property had been sold in 1915 and the North Family property four years later, with the remaining members joining the South Family.

On 10 March 1924 a letter from Elder Walter Shepherd of the Central Ministry of Mt. Lebanon had informed Eldresses Anna Case and Caroline L. Tate, as trustees at Watervliet, that a Mr. Thomas B. Bergan of Utica was prepared to exercise his option and purchase the Church Family farm. The property was sold to him for $60,000. A year later he resold the farm to the county of Albany for $160,000.

Four sisters, Libbie DeLong, Harriet Jones, Josephine Hewitt, and Julia McNallen, aging members of the Church Family, rebelled and refused to leave the old dwelling house. Sister Harriet must have eventually changed her mind, as a legal agreement written in 1927 begins with "Whereas, all the other members of said family except Libbie DeLong, Julia McNallen and Josephine Hewitt have joined the South Family."[77]

The sisters, who, according to a newspaper article, wanted their share of the purchase price of the North and Church Family properties, contended that they had not known about the sale. This is probably true since the ministry apparently handled the legalities.

According to the agreements signed by all parties, a sum in Shaker bank accounts amounting to approximately $2,500 was divided among the South Family and the remaining three Church Family members. There may have been similar agreements with the others, but we know only of the agreement between Sister Julia and Trustees Anna Case and Caroline Tate, in which the trustees agreed to give Sister Julia $25 a month for life or until she should ask to be

reinstated, and also agreed to bury her body in a suitable place and with suitable ceremonies. We do not know if Sister Julia ever applied for reinstatement, but she was buried at Watervliet in 1931 at the age of eighty-four.

On 15 April 1927 a spectacular fire, whipped by a strong wind, swept the model dairy farm of Leonard Bol, Sr. Within one hour thirteen buildings (the former North Family) had been consumed. Again in 1932 the same property (by then the Shaker Ridge Country Club) suffered another fire, destroying the last vestige of the Second Order of the Church Family at Wisdom's Valley. (This was the last of many serious fires which had plagued the Shaker community over the years. One of these fires was the reason for *The Shaker* newspaper's being moved to Mount Lebanon in 1873.) The Church Family property became the county hospital, or Ann Lee Home, in 1926. Many buildings were razed, and the remaining buildings were faced with brick, including the 1847 meeting-house, where the Groveland walnut benches for the world may still be seen in what is now the Catholic chapel of Saint Elizabeth's of Hungary.

Sister Lucy Bowers, who came from Enfield, Connecticut, was a fey little person, who taught the children about the stars and wrote the song "Courage." She recalled having had "very little chance for education. We had only 16 weeks schooling, and that was from May to September and I left school when 13 years old. Being born with an intense desire to learn, I used every means to add to my little stock of information."[78] As author of the 1928 South Family "Wanamaker Diary," she recorded with humor the historic change from Shaker village to county airport. A new dairy separator and a new herdsman, wood hauling and ice cutting, strawberry plants coming, and hayloads are part of the picture. "Ella and Mabel come out of the cook room, [and] Mary comes out of the Dining

---

This portrait of Eldress Anna Case taken in 1930 by William F. Winter personifies the Shakers' dedication to peace and perfection. Eldress Anna spent over seventy years of her life as a member of the South Family. (Nellie Oyer Winter Collection)

Room, . . . Ella . . . goes into Dining Room, [and] Lucy comes out . . . at noon," are lighthearted notes on the work rotation used to dispel boredom. Of Shaker hospitality the dairy records: "Seven men to dinner . . . Mr. & Mrs. Adams here . . . men still come from Airport to dinner . . . four officials come to dinner from the poor farm . . . ten men to dinner . . . Hazel came Feb. 26th and goes March 2 . . . Anna Lothridge comes to dinner . . . plenty of auto parties come and go . . . about thirty extra sheets to wash for company."

More interest was shown in the world: "all hands to the Airport all day, Hugo goes up in a ship . . . Democrat Convention closes, a week of talk, music and terrible demonstration . . . many airships are in the sky . . . go to the polls this am, vote for Hoover [This is the first reference to the Shakers voting; previously the Shakers did not vote or hold office.] . . . work at Airport still goes on with our tractor."

There was leisure time for radio and theatre: "The Cadman hour was splendid . . . McNamee announced the great ball game at the Rose Bowl . . . hear Clarence Darrow speak . . . Christmas Eve glorified with music from NYC Roxy Theatre . . . sisters go to Capitol Theatre to see 'The Vagabond King' . . . Eldress Anna, Grace and Caroline to Albany to see 'Abbie's Irish Rose' . . . send $3.38 by money order for 'Make 'Em Laugh.'"

And disappointment in the futility of the Shaker cause starts to become apparent: "nothing doing here . . . people come and go, but nothing doing . . . dreadful weather, but we take what we get. Man comes prepared to join the spiritual organization called Shakers — wow — wow — won't he be disappointed though . . . we look over old papers dating from 1832 and burn them."[79]

Neighbors, Shaker children, and authors of diaries have given accounts which make it possible to profile individual Shakers. Two were particularly memorable — the last male Shaker and the last eldress at Wisdom's Valley, Hamilton DeGraw and Anna Case.

Hamilton DeGraw, born in 1853, came to Watervliet from Groveland in 1892. He was beloved by all the children whose lives he touched. They remember him leaving melons at the gate for them to enjoy after school. Although legend says that he perfected hybrid corn for the Burpee Company, the only information we have is that he "sold back seed corn to the Burpee Company." A late newspaper picture of Brother Hamilton showed him listening to his Atwater Kent radio with a Landon button in his lapel. The children remember his allowing them to listen to Santa Claus on that radio and also to play with his pet gander, Tommy. He grew beautiful sweet peas, and there are legends that he sold vegetables to the neighbors for his own profit until the eldresses found out about it.

Anna Case, born in 1855, came to Watervliet as a child of twelve, and remained there for her entire life. She led an exemplary life among the Shakers. Everyone loved her, and she made a multitude of friends outside Shakerism. She was eldress at the South Family for many years.

The next-to-last male at the South Family was Byron Coburn. Born in 1873, he came to Watervliet from Groveland in 1892 and became a member of the North Family along with a natural brother and sister. As the photographs show, he engaged in many agricultural activities, being most remembered for raising chickens and tending honey bees. Apparently he either was in disfavor or temporarily left the Watervliet family about 1912 to live in Albany. He was never referred to as brother. He returned in later years and lived at the South Family, where more than one of the world's children remember his accuracy in forecasting the weather. Byron died in 1935 at the age of 62 and is buried in the Shaker burying ground.

In 1928 three girls who had been brought up from childhood by the Shakers left and went back to the world before they could sign the covenant on their twenty-first birthdays. Brother Hamilton DeGraw was the only remaining male. Besides Eldresses Anna Case and Caroline Tate, the remaining Shaker sisters were Jennie Wells, who had come to Watervliet with the Groveland Shakers in 1892 and who left and went to Mount Lebanon before 1938; Lucy Bowers, who died in 1935; Ella Winship, the schoolteacher, who had also come with the Groveland group and went from Watervliet to become an eldress at Mt. Lebanon; Anna Goepper, who was born in Germany in 1870 and died at Watervliet in 1937; and the last three to leave Watervliet, Freida Sipple and the natural sisters Grace and Mary Dahm.

Anna Goepper is remembered for her endearing sense of humor; the Cross sisters recall her comment that "you are Cross by name and not by nature." As keeper of the South Family daily journal in 1916 she notes on 17 November: "We had 16 men for dinner. I made 17 apple pies, 10 loaves bread, picked and cleaned 7 chickens, stewed pumpkin for pies, mashed and prepared it. I have been busy all day since four o'clock."[80]

The South Family was closed after the death of Eldress Anna Case on 18 July 1938. The three remaining sisters went to Mt. Lebanon, and the bell on the dwelling house was sounded for the last time at Wisdom's Valley.

Right: The last eldress's Watervliet Shaker School report card for 1869, two years after her arrival. Of the ten instances in which her grade fell short of Very Good, four are for Mental Arithmetic and two for Philosophy.

WATERVLIET SHAKER SCHOOL.

District No. 14.   Department No.

Attendance and Recitation of *Ann Case*

Commencing *July 27th 1869*

Schedules are to be signed by the Parents or Guardians, and punctually returned on the following Tuesday.

Laura Ann Printup Teacher.

5 signifies Very Good. 4 signifies Good. 3 signifies Medium. 2 signifies Poor. 1 signifies Very Poor. a signifies Absent.

	Reading	Spelling	Arithmetic	Mental Arith.	Geography	Writing	Grammar	Astronomy	Physiology	Philosophy	Composition	Conduct	Cleanliness	Attendance
M														
T	5	5	5	4	5	5	5					5	5	5
W	5	5	5		5	5	4	*Picnic*			5	5	5	
T	5	5	5	4	5	5	5					5	5	5
F	5	5	5		5	5	4	4		3		5	5	5
S	5		5									5	5	5
M														
T	5	5	5		5	5	5			3		5	5	5
W	5	5	5	3	5	5	5					5	5	5
T	5	5	5	5	5	5	5	5		5		5	5	5
F	5	5	5		5	5	5					5	5	5
S														
M														
T	5	5	5	5		5	5					5	5	5
W	5	5	5			5	5					4	5	5
T	5	5	5	4		5	5					5	5	5
F	5	5	5				5					5	5	5
S														
M														
T	5	5	5	5	5	5	5					5	5	5
W	5	5	5	5	5	5	5	5		5		5	5	5
T	5	5	5		5	5	5					5	5	5
F	5	5	5	5	5	5	5					5	5	5
S														

The six small panels above comprise a panoramic view of the Church Family taken by Edwin T. Stein in 1927, when the property was sold to Albany County but before some buildings were razed to convert the complex into the Ann Lee Home. From left to right, the major buildings in the two enlarged panels below are the herb and joiners shop (building date unknown), razed after 1927; brick shop (built 1822), still standing; second house (built 1790), razed 1927; stone shop (built in nineteenth century), razed 1927; first dwelling house (built 1818),

razed 1927; ministry shop (built 1825), still standing; first meetinghouse (built 1791), razed 1927; second meetinghouse (built 1846), still standing; and the brick trustees' office (built 1830) still standing. At the time the county was negotiating for the property the Odd Fellows of Eastern New York held an option on and considered the place as a home for old members. (New York State History Collection)

Left: *The West Family broom shop, believed to have been the family's first dwelling house erected in 1810, appears unused in this 1940 photograph by Nelson E. Baldwin — as does the seed house in the background. The broom shop has since been converted to an apartment building. (New York State History Collection)*

Left: *A 1973 photograph of the Ann Lee Home shows the remodeled Church Family buildings that remain — at left, the brick shop; obscured in the distance, the ministry shop; in the center, the second meetinghouse; and in the right foreground, the trustees' office. All of these buildings have been remodeled with brick facing, and some have also been provided with porches and dormers. (Historical Society of the Town of Colonie Collection)*

Below: *This 1930 view of the South Family shows the buildings seen from the barns with the bell house at the extreme right. (New York State History Collection)*

Left: *This photograph of Eldresses Rosetta Hendrickson and Anna Case at the South Family sauce and jelly house was taken in the early twentieth century. It is an obviously posed photograph, with the eldresses wearing the traditional costume with silk kerchiefs. The building was built in 1800 and razed ca. 1930. (New York State History Collection)*

Right: *Sisters Mary Dahm and Maggie Caldwell, photographed at the South Family ca. 1900. Sister Mary and her natural sister, Grace, were two of the last three survivors at the closing of the South Family in 1938. Sister Maggie is well remembered in the last years of the Shaker community, but it is believed that she left before the village closed. (Emma B. King Library, Shaker Museum, Old Chatham)*

Seated left to right, in this North Family group picture taken ca. 1915 are Sisters Ella Winship, Eldress Lavinia Dutcher, and an unidentified woman. Standing are Elder Hamilton DeGraw, Hattie Coburn (sister of Byron Coburn), and Sister Jennie Wells. (Reproduced courtesy of Gertrude Reno Sherburne)

Sister Lucy Bowers (left) is shown with Ella Winship, Eldress Lavinia Dutcher, and the Central Ministry at Mt. Lebanon. The balsam pillows advertised in the shop window were among a wide range of fancy goods sold there. (Emma B. King Library, Shaker Museum, Old Chatham)

Byron Coburn came to the Watervliet North Family from Groveland in 1892. He is pictured here on the North Family milk wagon in the early 1900s. (Reproduced courtesy of Gertrude Reno Sherburne)

At left, Byron Coburn and an unidentified helper are shown cutting crops in a ca. 1925 photograph. (Reproduced courtesy of Marian Curtis Kunz)

Eldress Ella Winship, the schoolteacher of District No. 14, came to the North Family from Groveland in 1892, moved to the South Family at the close of the North Family, and is pictured here at Mt. Lebanon, where she was called to become an eldress. (Reproduced courtesy of Marian Curtis Kunz)

Born in Manchester, England, Sister Mary Ann Ayers joined the South Family and died there in 1912 at the age of 92. This photograph was taken ca. 1910. (Reproduced courtesy of Francis Spoonogle)

Right: This modern view of the Shaker cemetery at Watervliet is from the Index of American Design files at the National Gallery of Art.

Retracing the past

The Millennial Laws decreed that all Shaker families should keep detailed chronological records of business and daily life, but today's historian is frustrated by the fact that in later years the Shakers destroyed many of these records.

At the turn of the century, two of the world's historians collected and preserved the history of Shakerism. J. P. MacLean published the first Shaker bibliography in 1905. Wallace H. Cathcart, former director of the Western Reserve Historical Society in Cleveland, Ohio, started actively collecting material for its library, and he was able to persuade Eldress M. Catherine Allen of Mt. Lebanon, a member of the Central Ministry, to direct a quantity of valuable books and manuscripts to Ohio. As a consequence, the bulk of Watervliet material, as well as a substantial collection from other Shaker communities, has been well preserved at the Western Reserve Historical Society Library.

In 1915, Eldress Catherine spent several weeks at Watervliet searching for material for Cathcart. In 1919 her correspondence with him tells us that she visited Watervliet again at the time the North Family was closing and selected material which she sent to him by express with the caution that "I prefer your use of [the] waste basket than the risk of disposing unwisely of that which may be of service in any place." She also mentioned that "Eldress Anna Case is always pleased with your kind remembrance of her and will be glad when you can again find time to be a guest of the family over which she presides."[81]

A 1920 letter from Sister Ella Winship at Watervliet also complimented Mr. Cathcart: "The work of preserving the history of the Shaker organization is greatly appreciated by those of us who have any con-

ception of it, and we know this is but a small part of the whole."[82]

Following the tragic fire which destroyed so much of the former North Family property in 1926, Mrs. La-Grange Spicer of Cohoes sent a letter to the Office of State History with a small box of Shaker cut nails retrieved from the fire, insisting that something be done to preserve the Shaker history. The county of Albany had just purchased the Church Family property, where they eventually built the Ann Lee Home for the county poor, a million-dollar county jail, and a flying field. In the same year, Dr. Charles C. Adams had become the director of the New York State Museum. In Dr. Adams's own words, "The destruction and modification of these [Church Family] buildings made available, through the courtesy of the local county officials, a large amount of historic material illustrating the history and industries of the Shakers."[83]

Mr. William L. Lassiter, then Assistant State Botanist, was appointed by Dr. Adams as curator of the Shaker project. An author and collector, he befriended the members of the Watervliet South Family, and it was he who rang the last bell at the close of the Watervliet community.

During the formation of the New York State Shaker collection valuable assistance was given by Faith and Edward Deming Andrews, Shaker scholars who had started their own famous collection in 1923. Dr. Adams appointed Dr. Andrews as temporary curator of history, in which post Andrews wrote *The Community Industries of the Shakers* which focused on Mt. Lebanon and Watervliet.

William F. Winter made a major contribution to the New York State Shaker collection with his superb photographs of the Shakers, their architecture, furniture, and tools. Working with both Dr. Adams and Dr. Andrews, he was given an open invitation by the Shakers to visit and photograph whenever he desired. With what he called his Shaker portfolio he left an

---

In the extreme right foreground of this 1963 aerial photograph is the Ann Lee Pond, and across the road, the Shaker cemetery; the Ann Lee Home (the former Church Family property) is above the cemetery. The Albany County Airport is in the center of the photograph. (New York State Department of Transportation)

unequalled historical record of Shakerism.

Another professional record, the Historic American Building Survey, was made during the 1930s and 1940s under the direction of the United States Department of the Interior, National Park Service. It consists of eighty sheets of measured drawings of the Watervliet West and South Families.

From a very modest beginning in 1928, when construction started at the Albany County airport with the Shakers' tractor, there have been many stages of development culminating in the present modern airport on the grounds where the Watervliet Shakers first set foot two hundred years ago.

The Albany Airport opened officially with an air meet, which the Shakers attended, between 3 and 7 October. The Air Mail Field Post Office was established there on 1 November 1928.

Beneath the runway is the first resting place of the founder of Shakerism, Mother Ann Lee, who died in 1784. Along with that of her brother, Father William Lee, and that of one of the first converts to Shakerism, her body was reinterred to rest finally in the community cemetery in 1835.

Over the years the Shakers have tried to maintain the cemetery according to the rules set by the Central Ministry in 1872, with more or less success. Today, the maintenance of the cemetery is shared through mutual agreement between the Town of Colonie and the Shaker Parent Ministry (formerly Central Ministry) which still owns the Watervliet Shaker cemetery. The present Shaker Parent Ministry is composed of Eldresses Gertrude Soule and Bertha Lindsay, who represent the two extant communities of Shakers at Sabbathday Lake, Maine, and Canterbury, New Hampshire. There are twelve Shaker sisters remaining in these two societies today.

Perhaps a word of warning for the scholar, the history student, and the just plain curious is in order here. The cemetery is all that remains of Wisdom's Valley to be seen by the visiting public. At present, only a glimpse of the buildings can be seen from the road.

The North Family is gone; what remains of the Church Family, owned by Albany County, is now the Ann Lee Home and Hospital; and the remains of the West and South Families are privately owned. Until the time when there might be a change in ownership for the purpose of historic preservation, the privacy of the land owners should be observed.

A prospect for the future

A Shaker presence remains in Colonie. Three clusters of twenty-seven historic buildings and some 770 acres of open farm and woodland attest to the recent past of Shaker communal and religious life. All of these structures and most of the land has been declared a national landmark and placed on the United States National Register of Historic Places and Sites.

The following illustrations present a means to create a variety of significant amenities at the center of the Town of Colonie, a once-in-a-lifetime chance to reuse, conserve, and preserve; to claim needed open space; to create forever wild areas around ponds; to provide nature walks through woods and wetlands; to establish a living historic core before the town's history is lost, and reuse the best Shaker buildings for needed contemporary purposes; to develop a variety of active and passive recreation facilities. All of this is possible, a living continuity for the public as an outgrowth of the Shakers' communal past.

The illustrations are summary diagrams of a major social, physical, political, and economic planning effort between 1973 and 1975, supported by the Town of Colonie, the Colonie Conservation Advisory Council, the Historical Society of the Town of Colonie, and the New York State Council on the Arts, and assisted by the New York State Office for Historic Preservation. The work was undertaken on their behalf by Dr. Peter Wolf, planning consultant in New York City and chairman of the Institute for Architecture and Urban Studies.

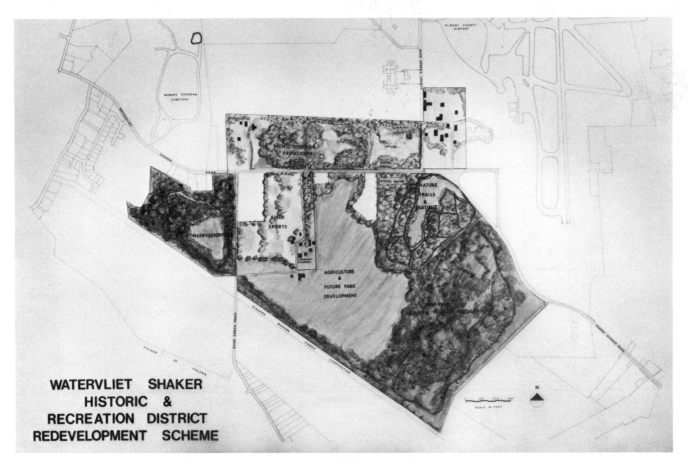

**WATERVLIET SHAKER
HISTORIC &
RECREATION DISTRICT
REDEVELOPMENT SCHEME**

The drawing above shows one possible redevelopment scheme. A unique preservation district of 580 acres is defined at the center of Colonie. Three clusters of extant Shaker buildings (which appear here as dark rectangles) are incorporated and preserved. Open farm and woodland threatened by conventional commercial and industrial development are reserved for public use and enjoyment. Ponds, forever wild woods, nature trails and hiking zones, agricultural areas, bicycle and jogging paths, picnic pavilions, small courts, and game areas surround the preserved buildings. The district is served by excellent road access. It is connected internally by bicycle paths and walking trails, which also link to the extended Colonie bicycle path system.

123

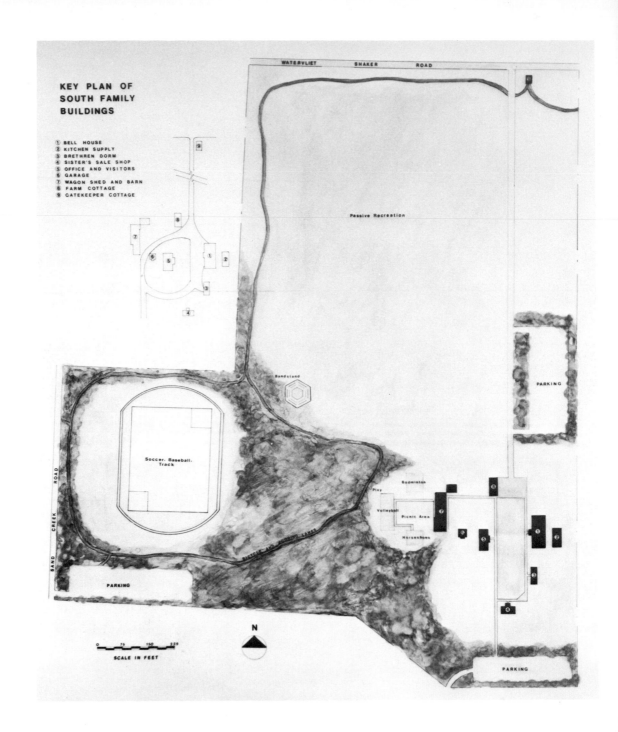

KEY PLAN OF
SOUTH FAMILY
BUILDINGS

① BELL HOUSE
② KITCHEN SUPPLY
③ BRETHREN DORM
④ SISTER'S SALE SHOP
⑤ OFFICE AND VISITORS
⑥ GARAGE
⑦ WAGON SHED AND BARN
⑧ FARM COTTAGE
⑨ GATEKEEPER COTTAGE

WATERVLIET   SHAKER   ROAD

Passive Recreation

Bandstand

Soccer. Baseball.
Track

PARKING

Badminton

Play

Volleyball   Picnic Area

Horseshoes

SAND CREEK ROAD

BICYCLE AND JOGGING LANES

PARKING

PARKING

0   75   150   225
SCALE IN FEET

N

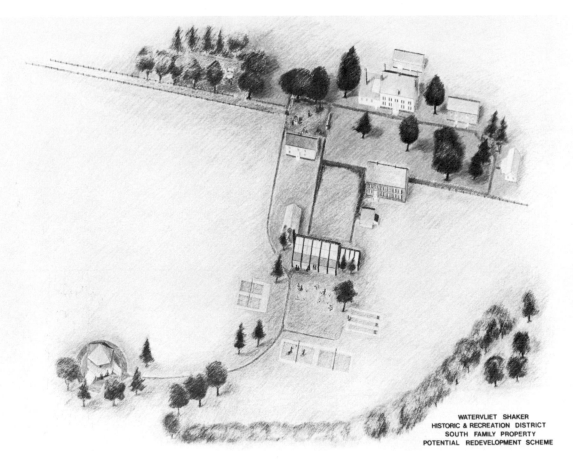

WATERVLIET SHAKER
HISTORIC & RECREATION DISTRICT
SOUTH FAMILY PROPERTY
POTENTIAL REDEVELOPMENT SCHEME

The project could start right away. Acquisition of the South Family property is the key. It lies between and links each of the other parcels still in private ownership. The state of New York has already allocated funds for purchase of historic structures on the property. The federal government is in advanced stages of project review. Local approval for matching funds is necessary to implement the planned land acquisition program. After land acquisition, the most important of the original Shaker buildings would be restored. Possible contemporary uses include museum, meeting center,

craft shop, display area, and offices for town or nonprofit organizations. In addition, there is a suggested outdoor bandstand and a multipurpose and multiseason recreational field for soccer, baseball, and track. Most of the land is reserved as open space.

The view above shows the redeveloped central area of the South Family property. Historic buildings, clustered around a green, require only minor interior adjustments and exterior reconditioning. Through traffic is eliminated. (Peripheral parking is provided.) The barn pavilion

terrace overlooks children's play and barbecue areas surrounded by badminton, volleyball, and horseshoe courts. Further along the walk, a new bandstand is planned for summer theatre, concerts, and community celebrations.

Bibliography

This section includes both sources of text quotations and major references. Numbers correspond to the superior figures used throughout the text. Manuscript items have been coded:

(AIHA)   Albany Institute of History and Art, Albany, N.Y.
(COL)   Historical Society of the Town of Colonie, N.Y.
(EBK)   Emma B. King Library, Shaker Museum, Old Chatham, N.Y.
(LC)   Library of Congress, Washington, D.C.
(NYSH)   New York State History Collection, Rotterdam, N.Y.
(NYSL)   New York State Library, Albany, N.Y.
(PITT)   Berkshire Athenaeum, Pittsfield, Mass.
(PRI)   Private collections.
(SHHS)   Shaker Heights Historical Society, Cleveland, Ohio.
(SABB)   United Society of Shakers, Sabbathday Lake, Maine.
(WCL)   Williams College, Williamstown, Mass.
(WIN)   Henry Francis duPont Winterthur Museum, Winterthur, Del.
(WRHS)   Western Reserve Historical Society, Cleveland, Ohio.

1. *Funk & Wagnall's New Standard Dictionary of the English Language*, 1913, s.v. "legend."

2. Prudence Morrill, "Account of a Journey by Prudence Morrill and Eliza Sharp," 1847 (EBK).

3. W. J. Haskett, *Shakerism Unmasked* (Pittsfield, 1828), p. 30.

4. Diaries of Donald MacDonald, 1824 (EBK).

5. D. A. Buckingham, "List of Decayed Buildings," ca. 1825 (WRHS).

6. Victor Hugo Paltsits, ed., *Minutes of the Commissioners for detecting and defeating Conspiracies in the State of New York* (Albany, 1910), pp. 469, 504.

7. Margot Mayo, "The Incredible Journey of Mother Ann," *The Shaker Quarterly* 2 (Spring 1962): 42–52.

8. Joel Munsell, *Annals of Albany*, 2d. ed. (Albany: J. Munsell, 1869), 2: 288.

9. William Spence Robinson, ed., "The Diary of Francisco de Miranda, tour of the United States, 1783–1784," *The Hispanic Society of America* (1928), p. 201.

10. Louis Gottschalk, *LaFayette Between the American and the French Revolution* (Chicago: University of Chicago Press, 1965), 4: 107.

11. St. John Honeywood, *Poems, with some Pieces in Prose* (New York: T & Y Swords, 1801), p. 141.

12. Albany County Tax List, 1786 (NYSL).

13. U. S. Census, 1790, p. 52.

14. Thomas Brown, *An Account of the People Called Shakers* . . . (Troy: Parker & Bliss, 1812), p. 58.

15. D. A. Buckingham, "Epitomic History of the Watervliet Shakers," *The Shaker* 7 (July 1877), 49–50.

16. Walter Geer, ed., *Recollections of the Revolution and Empire* (New York: Brentano's, 1920), p. 214.

17. Geer, *Recollections,* p. 216.

18. Moses Guest, *Poems on Several Occasions* . . . (Cincinnati: Looker & Reynolds, 1823), p. 121.

19. Brown, *Account,* pp. 14, 20, 70.

20. Brown, *Account,* p. 28.

21. *Laws of New York,* 1797–1800, vol. 4.

22. Albany County Clerk, Book of Deeds, No. 17, p. 326.

23. Brown, *Account,* p. 58.

24. Issachar Bates, "Sketch of the Life and Experience of Issachar Bates," 1833 (EBK).

25. Anna White and Leila S. Taylor, *Shakerism: Its Meaning and Message* (Columbus, 1904), p. 111.

26. Timothy Dwight, *Travels in New-England and New-York* (London, 1821–3), 3: 149.

27. "Records of the South Family," 1800–1845 (NYSL).

28. *A Declaration of The Society of People (commonly called Shakers) shewing Their Reasons for Refusing To Aid or Abet the Cause of War and Bloodshed* . . . (Albany: E. & E. Hosford, 1815) (PITT).

29. *The Memorial of James Chapman to the respectable Legislature of the State of New York.* (Albany, 1817) (NYSL).

30. Thomas Jefferson, *The Writings of Thomas Jefferson,* ed. Andrew Lipscomb (Washington, D.C.: Thomas Jefferson Memorial Assn., 1903) 15: 134.

31. *Indoctum Parliamentum: A Farce in One Act and a Beautiful Variety of Scenes* (n.p., n.d.).

32. *Petition to New York State Legislature relative to Militia Fines,* 1823 (NYSL).

33. "Autobiography of Martin Van Buren," *American Historical Association Annual Report* (1918) 2: 153–4.

34. Joel Munsell, *Annals of Albany,* 1st ed. (Albany: J. Munsell, 1850), 8: 97.

35. Munsell, *Annals,* 1st ed., 5: 238.

36. J. Milbert, *Picturesque Itinerary of the Hudson River, and the Peripheral Parts of North America* (New Jersey: Gregg Press, 1968), pp. 43–44.

37. Benjamin S. Youngs, David Darrow, and Joseph Meacham, *Testimony of Christ's Second Appearing* (Albany: E. & E. Hosford, 1810).

38. Theodore Johnson, "The Millennial Laws of 1860," *The Shaker Quarterly* 11 (Winter 1971).

39. Seth Wells, "Mother Lucy's Last Visit to Watervliet," 1821 (WRHS).

40. Diaries of Donald MacDonald, 1824 (EBK).

41. James Fenimore Cooper, *The Traveling Bachelor* (New York: Stringer and Townsend, 1852), pp. 247–50.

42. Jefferson, *Writings,* 15: 399.

43. Covenant of the Young Believers Order, 1830–1912 (EBK).

44. "Records of the South Family," 1800–1845 (NYSL).

45. George W. Pierson, *Tocqueville and Beaumont in America* (New York: Oxford University Press, 1938), pp. 178–79.

46. Herman Melville, *Moby Dick; or The Whale* (Rhinehart, 1948), p. 311.

47. "The Shakers," *Niles Weekly Register*, reprinted *Boston Palladium*, 19 September 1829.

48. Journal of Elias Raub, 1837 (PRI).

49. Munsell, *Annals*, 1st ed., 9: 316–25.

50. "Church Family Journal," 1837–49 (NYSL).

51. John Bigelow, *The Life of Samuel J. Tilden* (New York: Harper & Bros., 1895), p. 80.

52. "Fifteen Years A Shakeress," *Galaxy* 13 (January–April 1872): 31–37.

53. Robert F. W. Meader, "Zion Patefacta," *The Shaker Quarterly* 2 (Spring 1962): 5–17.

54. Paulina Bates, *The Divine Book of Holy and Eternal Wisdom* (Canterbury, N.H., 1849), p. 696.

55. "Narrative of James Wardley, Jr. Seen and wrote down in vision by Phebe Ann Smith of Watervliet March 4th, 1839," from A Collection of Hymns, Anthems & Tunes; Adapted to the Worship. By the Singers at South Union, Ky., April 4th, 1835 (PRI).

56. "Public Notice, October 22, 1847" (WRHS).

57. Munsell, *Annals*, 1st ed., 5: 275.

58. Munsell, *Annals*, 1st ed., 5: 275.

59. S. N. Beers and D. G. Beers, *New Topographical Atlas of the Counties of Albany and Schenectady, New York* (Philadelphia: Stone & Stewart, 1866), p. 31.

60. "Appointment of Committee for Repair of Buildings," 1851 (WRHS).

61. "Stipulations Relative to Divisions of Real Estate," 1860 (EBK).

62. "A Peep at Shakerdom," *Frank Leslie's Illustrated Newspaper*, 11 January 1873.

63. "Church Family Journal," 1837–49 (NYSL).

64. Munsell, *Annals*, 1st ed., 6: 342.

65. Munsell, *Annals*, 1st ed., 9: 336.

66. Mrs. Charles Hamlin, "The United Society of Believers Known as the Shakers . . .," 1951 (AIHA).

67. Boler, Avery, Gates, and Miller to Sacks, Fox, Kiewar, and Rapahoo Indians, 1874 (WRHS).

68. John Noyes, *History of American Socialism* (Philadelphia: Lippincott & Co., 1870), p. 669.

69. Charles Nordhoff, *The Communistic Societies of the United States* (New York: Harper & Bros., 1875), p. 117.

70. Charles D. Warner, "Visit to Watervliet," *Scribner's Monthly* 18 (August 1879): 554.

71. "Burying Ground Directions," 27 April 1880 (WRHS).

72. Warner, "Visit to Watervliet," pp. 552, 557.

73. Munsell, *Annals*, 2nd ed., 2: 346.

74. Elizabeth Reid, "A Trip to Shaker Settlement, 1887" (SHHS).

75. Giles B. Avery, "Programme of Eastern Journey," 1886 (WRHS).

76. Second Family, "A Family Journal," 1885–1894 (WCL).

77. "Agreement between Trustees of the United Society and Church of Believers with Julia McNallen, 1927," Stedman Papers (COL).

78. Lucy S. Bowers, "Memorial Tribute to Sister Sarah Copley" (WCL).

79. South Family, "The Wanamaker Diary," 1928 (PRI).

80. "South Family Journal," 1915–1916 (NYSL).

81. Allen to Cathcart, 1919, Wallace H. Cathcart Collection (WRHS).

82. Winship to Cathcart, 1920, Wallace H. Cathcart Collection (WRHS).

83. Edward Deming Andrews, *The Community Industries of the Shakers*, New York State Museum Handbook No. 15 (Albany: University of the State of New York, 1933), p. 4.

84. Andrews, *Community Industries*.

The following references have been consulted extensively in the preparation of this publication but not cited in the text:

Manuscripts

Albany. New York State Library. Land and Personal Tax Lists of the N.W. Quarter of the Manor of Ranselaer District. 1779.

Albany. New York State Library. Map of Church Family [by John J. McManus, Albany County surveyor, 1926].

Albany. New York State Library. New York State Census. 1790, 1800, 1810, 1820, 1830, 1840, 1850, 1860, 1870, 1880, 1892, 1905.

Albany. New York State Library. Tax List. 24 October 1788.

Albany. New York State Library. Van Rensselaer papers. Book A, Part 1. West Manor Ledger.

Albany. Office of County Clerk. Book of Deeds. Nos. 17, 18, 19, 28, 29, 38, 41, 57, 58, 64, 67, 81, 83, 86, 87, 88, 92, 98, 100, 117, 120, 143, 157, 166, 182, 353.

Cleveland. Western Reserve Historical Society. Account Book of Strawberry Plants. 1859.

Cleveland. Western Reserve Historical Society. Explanation of maintenance of aged and infirm. 1825.

Cleveland. Western Reserve Historical Society. Map of the Spiritual City of the Valley of Wisdom and Survey, Holy City, Wisdom's Valley [Evert Van Alen, surveyor]. 1842.

Cleveland. Western Reserve Historical Society. Records of the South House, Watervliet. 1823–31.

Colonie. Historical Society of the Town of Colonie, N.Y. Search of Watervliet Shaker Deeds [by R. Arthur Johnson]. 1975.

Colonie. Historical Society of the Town of Colonie, N.Y. Unpublished research of Alvin P. Boettcher.

Private Collection. "Groveland, New York." [by G. J. Doolittle, M.D.].

Williamstown, Mass. Williams College. West Family diary, 1894–98.

Laws of New York

Laws of New York. 1797–1800, 1816, 1818, 1824, 1839, 1849, 1852, 1896.

McKinney's Consolidated Laws of New York. Book 50, Religious Corporations Law.

McKinney's Consolidated Laws of New York. Book 22, General Corporations Law.

McKinney's Consolidated Laws of New York. Book 14, Domestic Relations Law.

Books

Andrews, Edward Deming. *The People Called Shakers.* New York: Oxford University Press, 1953.

Becker, Howard I. "Ca-Nas-Ta-Gi-O-Ne," 1968.

MacLean, J. P. *A Bibliography of Shaker Literature.* 1905. Reprint. New York: Burt Franklin, 1971.

Melcher, Marguerite Fellows. *The Shaker Adventure.* Cleveland: Case Western Reserve University Press, 1968.

New York State Museum. *The New York State Museum's Historical Survey and Collection of the New York Shakers.* Albany: University of the State of New York, 1941.

U.S., Library of Congress. *National Union Catalog.*

Periodicals

Blake, Nelson M. "Eunice Against the Shakers." *New York State History,* October 1960.

Cushman, Charlotte. "Lines: . . . a visit to the Shaker Settlement. . . ." *Knickerbocker,* January 1837.

Gilreath, James W. "The Formation of the Western Reserve Historical Society's Shaker Collection." *Journal of Library History, Philosophy, and Comparative Librarianship* 8 (1973).

"Legislature of New York." *Niles Weekly Register.* 29 March 1817.

Peladeau, Marius B. "The Shaker Meetinghouses of Moses Johnson." *Antiques,* October 1970.

Poppeliers, John. "Shaker Architecture and the Watervliet South Family." *New York State History,* January 1966.

U.S., Congress. *Annals of Congress.* 1824.

Photograph credits

The author is indebted to the following photographers for works reproduced here:

Roland K. Alexander: page 120. Harry A. Bigelman: pages 17, 21, 22 r., 23, 24, 39, 41, 45, 46, 47, 54 top and bottom r., 55 top, 56, 58, 61, 64 top, 66, 67, 68, 75 l., 76 bottom, 77, 84, 88, 89 top, 90 r., 95 bottom, 109. James Bourne: page 112 top. Kenneth Hay: 18. Lee's Studio: 59 top, 85, 91 r., 115, 116 bottom. Elmer R. Pearson: 71, 80, 83. David Serette: 64 bottom.

This ca. 1850–75 chair in the collection of the Philadelphia Museum of Art was owned by Eldresses Josephine Wilson, Rosetta Stephens, and Anna Case according to museum records.